The Bunch Book of Selling

of Selling

How to Sell a Bunch...Not a Little

By
AUSTIN W. BUNCH

The World According to Austin Bunch

Nothing in this book is untested or just conjecture. It is a sharing of what I have learned through trial and error in front of my customers.

Many ideas will resonate, while others will be new to many. A few will bring back what you know that you have forgotten you had.

Many ideas are invitations to growth. Ideas that force you to dig deeper into yourself, to be open to discovering new strengths and opportunities to becoming an outstanding sales specialist.

Putting these ideas to the test in front of your customers will differentiate you from the many common salespeople.

Foreword

In my five decades in the gift and home industry, I have been a retailer, a salesperson, a sales manager and a president of a large supplier that employed more than 200 direct salespeople. As such I have seen the performances of salespeople and sales from every perspective possible.

I first came to know Austin Bunch while I was president of a large gift and home company called CBK Ltd. I was immediately impressed with his vast knowledge of detailed sales and sales training techniques, combined with his long-term knowledge of this industry, from helping run companies to his product development expertise.

After working with him as a consultant I convinced him to join CBK as a vice president. We worked together until our ownership team sold the company and I started a consulting company of my own. Since then, I have recommended Austin to dozens of my clients over the years and every single one of them has been amazed at the results he produces.

Austin quickly became – and remains so to this day – the industry leader in building in-house tele-sales teams that have been proven to reach more customers while increasing both sales and profit margins and, at the same time, reducing costs. No one else in this industry comes close to doing what he does for hiring and training people in how to sell on the telephone as well as in-person in company showrooms. In fact, potential clients will wait until he is available, that's how singular he is in this business.

His dedication to his craft is legendary.

If you have been fortunate enough to be a client of Austin's, this book will be a welcome trip through familiar territory. And if you have not worked with Austin, then take advantage of the lessons he has learned and taught to multiple companies and individuals whose careers, successes and lives have been enhanced by their time with this man.

Randy Eller
President
Eller Enterprises LLC
Sorrento, FL

Testimonials

"Back in the recent downturn, we knew it would be a hard storm to weather but instead of scaling back and panicking we hired Austin Bunch. We thought he could put into place a unique marketing program that would at least keep our heads above water. But what occurred instead was that business rose well above our expectations and we flourished, having the biggest sales years in our business history.

"We are only sorry we did not start with Austin sooner. We truly believe that outside sales reps are a thing of the past and if you want to keep up with the ever-changing landscape of the industry you need to change your ways, move fast and reach more customers on a daily basis. Having a dedicated team for your company is the way to do this.

"Change is the key word."

Doug Williams
President
Kalalou

"Austin's knowledge is insurmountable and I learned a tremendous amount from his training. His process of training the team still rings true with them years later. I continue to hear, 'Well, Austin taught us!'"

Teresa Roberts
Director of Sales
Jaipur Living

"Every team within every sport has a coach and a playbook to instruct his players on where to be, how to perform and what each team member must be doing concisely to produce a positive result from a play. It's no different for a sales team. Every member needs the tools, which are the scripts, the planning and preparation to become successful individually as well as a team."

Steve Moniz
Vice President of Sales
Zodax

"Being a word nerd and having a love of the English language, I found the training to be of great interest. To see how much of a positive reaction can come from the way in which we string together a sentence or change it slightly was so interesting. The most valuable phrase I have put into practice is 'May I.' I find this to be incredibly effective. I have seen it consistently calm an apprehensive customer and allow for a mutually beneficial conversation to be held. I found the training to be exceptionally valuable with respect to language, scripting, tone and the further development of listening skills.

"The second most valuable tool I took away was the 'If I had to do the call over again, what would I do differently?' This has positively impacted on my daily calls and I find myself asking the same question outside of the office as well.

"The tools Austin shared have positively impacted both my personal and professional life. "

Christine Lynch
Inside Sales Specialist
Audrey Co.

Meet Austin W. Bunch

A ustin W. Bunch began his selling career at age 19 when he put some samples in the trunk of his $150 used Ford and started knocking on doors, selling pots and pans. He said on that first day, he drove around the block five times before he had the courage to knock on his first door.

But he made the sale that day and he hasn't looked back since. Over a career that spans more than 60 years he has sold everything from household goods like that cookware to toys to jewelry even to pantyhose. You'll have to read the book to see how he tried on that pantyhose to make the sale, but no matter what he was selling he discovered the process was remarkably similar.

And, after selling literally hundreds of millions of dollars' worth of goods, that path took Austin from salesman to teacher and that's what he's been doing ever since. Along the way he's developed a process that shows others how to do it as well as he has. And it works.

Austin is supposed to be retired these days but there's retirement and then there's Austin Bunch retirement. He still takes on clients and special projects and seems to be about as busy as ever. That doesn't mean he and his wife Marion, who live in Atlanta with their two rescue dogs, don't find time to enjoy life, travel and the good things. He's deserved it, for sure.

Table of Contents

Introduction

S o, it was one of my first sales calls and I was calling on a very big shoe chain with thousands of stores. The buyer was a tough industry maven. I started showing her my line, asking what she liked and what she thought she should buy.

"Damn son," she said as she put her elbows on her desk, lit a cigarette and started blowing smoke all over the room, including at me. "I thought you knew about pantyhose. Why are you asking me all these questions?"

I caught my breath and said, "Yes ma'am, you need this many in this color for each store."

I wrote up the very large order and left, not just with the order but with the knowledge that instead of asking what my customer needed, I should be telling her what she needed to buy from me. That's what was in it for me.

What's in it for you?

Yes, this is one more book about sales and selling. Whether you've been selling for 20 years or 20 minutes, you have your own experiences, ideas and theories about how to do your job.

"Selling is all about good communication."

Many of them are just plain wrong. And that's why what's in this book is what's in it for you.

I'm Austin Bunch and while I've spent my entire career selling, leading salesforces and training people how to sell, that alone isn't enough to get you to read this. What's important is that I've developed a process – The Bunch Book of Selling – that is both proven and easy to understand and adapt to your career. I call it "A Process to Success," the what, how-to and why in selling.

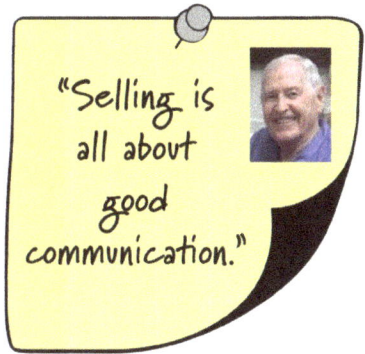

Understanding the selling process with hands-on and practical information that will allow you to sell better — and make more money — isn't rocket science. But it is science and like any good Selling 101 course, learning the basics and how to apply them every day isn't all that difficult.

"I learned that time and money were my real competitors. When I was in front of that customer, I was going to get everything they had to spend on the products I had."

I should know. I've sold hundreds of millions of dollars' worth of goods over my career and trained hundreds of people, from the smallest company to large Fortune 500 corporations to learn from me – my successes as well as my mistakes – to get to the point where I could write this book.

Sometimes a mistake can lead to a success. I was calling on a gift company called Kalalou trying to get them interested in using me as a sales advisor but not getting very far. One day, the owner, Doug Williams, finally told me, "Austin, you're a nice fellow but I am never going to use a consultant, please take me off your mailing and call list."

Doug caught me at a low point and so I did what he said and stopped calling on him. But a few months later a mutual friend who had done some work with Kalalou asked me if I was working with Doug. The company was having sales problems and my friend thought I could help.

I called Doug and he basically said, "Austin, gosh, I forgot all about you. I need help with sales, how quickly can you get here?"

At the first trade show I worked for the company we broke all sales records to the tune of a 150% increase. And we only went up from there.

I ended up working with Doug's company for many years, learning that you should never give up...and never believe everything a customer tells you.

"My tenacity came from the fact that I was a husband and father of five kids working on commission and I had to make every call pay."

I'm not a motivator. I learned early on I didn't have that power. A person is either motivated or they are not. But what I did have is what we all have: the dangerous ability to demotivate. I can teach, inspire, prod, lead and get out of the way and ultimately those are more important than just about anything.

All of this was the furthest thing from my mind when, at age 19, I began selling pots and pans door-to-door out of my $150 used Ford. I was terrified on my first sales call and must have driven around the block five times before I got out of the car and summoned up the courage to knock on that first front door.

But I made that sale and a lot more. Before too long I was both selling and training others at the company to sell. I had some great mentors – some not-so-great ones too – and became one of the company's top sellers.

From pots and pans I moved on to other consumer products: hosiery, handbags, jewelry, garden accessories, gifts, home décor accessories and toys, among other products. What I discovered was that regardless of what you were selling the process of selling remained remarkably consistent. And if you could find a way to define that process, script it and dissect the parts of it, you could teach others.

"I believe you must erase and replace to become a good sales consultant."

And that's what I've been doing for much of the past several decades. I've focused on business-to-business telesales but really much of what I offer can be applied to many different selling applications. I truly believe that once you learn how to sell over the telephone you can take those skills and sell in any situation, be it in-person at a trade show or market event or on the road.

Take pantyhose. When I first started selling one-size-fits-all hose, I was calling on a small chain of stores in the Louisville area and the buyer had one of his employees try on a pair to see if they really would fit all. She was only 5"2' and when she tried them on she came back and said they were a little tight in certain areas.

She left and I said to the buyer, "Give me those damn hose." I went into the bathroom and came out with them on my six-foot, 185-pound body and told the buyer, "if they fit me, they will fit her and 90% of the women out there. Now write the order."

And he did.

I'm not suggesting dressing up in women's clothing will always result in a sale but this book is all about telling you how to do it, not just stories about how I did it. It's not a rah-rah "you can do it" book but a kind of a mirror for the reader to discover some of the things they are doing that can be improved upon and learning some new things that work for a lot of a successful salespeople.

It's about differentiation, how to make you and what you're selling stand out from the rest of the pack. It's not just being priced a penny or two below the competition, even with a commodity product. I read in a business book – I read lots of business books all the time – "We live in a 'Surplus Society.'" A surplus of similar companies, employing similar people who have similar educational backgrounds, coming up with similar ideas and producing similar results.

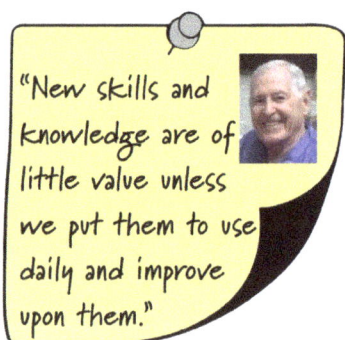

"New skills and knowledge are of little value unless we put them to use daily and improve upon them."

So, it's also about differentiating this book from the dozens – hell, hundreds – of other books on selling out there. The training here is to teach you selling skills and techniques to get maximum results in the shortest amount of time, providing transactional skills to quickly get your customers' attention and direct them to being engaged so they will take action on your information.

One of my best managers once asked me soon after I started working for him how much I wanted to make. I told him how much and he said, you will either make more or less. "I suggest you shoot for more."

It's that simple...and that's what's in it for you.

Start Smart

Chapter 1

Birth Of A Sales Consultant

A sales consultant is probably the most misunderstood profession in America. We're going to try to change that.

I define a Sales Consulant – it's a better name than sales specialist, don't you think? – as "a knowledgeable, organized business professional, respected by customers, who generates revenue through the selling of products and services."

If we asked a random person on the street the question: *"When you think about a sales consultant, what is the first product that comes to mind that he/she might sell?"* The majority will say cars, insurance, or vacuum cleaners. Two reasons they answer that way: 1. Most people do not consider sales a highly respected profession. 2. They think that just anyone can do sales and that selling does not require a lot of thought, learning or skill.

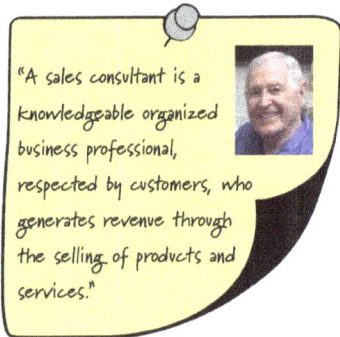

"A sales consultant is a knowledgeable organized business professional, respected by customers, who generates revenue through the selling of products and services."

In many cases, that is true for a large majority of car salespeople, store clerks, counter sales, route sales and many other sales jobs. However, that is just not true for medical sales, industrial sales, home and gift, heavy equipment, software, pharmacy, industrial real estate, stocks and bonds, etc. The list of high earners, well-educated and highly respected salespeople is very long.

This training will prepare you to be among highly respected salespeople and to earn a very good income in any sales position. So be prepared to be challenged and stretched outside your comfort zone. You are going to learn skills, techniques and a process for applying them.

It is also about making sales on purpose rather than by chance.

The very first thing you need to accomplish is to redefine what is a good sales consultant. First, this is what good sales consultants *are not*: They are not pushy salespeople only trying to sell something to a prospective customer just to make a sale. What we are and what you will become is a well-educated, knowledgeable company marketing and sales specialist. You will be assisting customers and prospects in having *the right products and service, at the right time, and at the right price.* You will become skilled and proficient in accomplishing this in a professional direct manner.

Five types of salespeople are described in the book *The Challenger Sale*, by Matthew Dixon and Brent Adamson.

1. <u>The Hard Worker:</u> Always willing to go the extra mile. Doesn't give up easily. Self-motivated. Interested in feedback and development. Concerned with making a good impression and less likely to quickly move the customer along.

2. <u>The Relationship Builder:</u> Builds strong advocates in customer organizations. Generous in giving time to help others. Gets along with everyone. Many times, uncomfortable in being assertive when the need is required.

3. <u>The Lone Wolf:</u> Follows own instincts. Self-assured. Makes a lot of sales but leaves all the details to others. Difficult to control and can alienate the customers.

4. <u>The Reactive Problem Solver:</u> Reliably responds to internal and external stakeholders. Ensures that all problems are solved. Detail oriented. Wants to do everything for the customer, even things that customer service should do.

5. <u>The Challenger:</u> Always has a different view of the world. Understands the customer's business. Loves to debate. Pushes the customer to think proactively. The Challenger is assertive, not passive, in talking with the customers. Takes less time to get the job done and move to the next customer/prospect.

The art of selling is not a negative or demeaning profession when properly understood and applied: We are in the business of helping customers make informed decisions by presenting them with qualified and quantified facts so that they can decide that our products and services will be of maximum benefit to them. We also help them discover that making decisions and finalizing the sale is to their benefit.

This book is about how to be a Challenger sales consultant.

Bunch's Tips To Success:

1. Think of the best sales consultant you've ever met.
2. Think of the worst sales consultant.
3. Evaluate the sales consultant that you are.

Chapter 2

The Transactional Sales Process

I advocate that of the five types of sales consultants noted in the previous section, the Challenger is the ideal sales consultant. Now, this may cause some misunderstanding until you learn *why your customers prefer this type of sales consultant.* We will be learning how to become a Challenger sales consultant and why it is very important in the **transactional** sales process. Challengers are assertive (not pushy), and they tend to press and assist the customers in their thinking and to take action.

The Challenger has many of the traits of the other four but gets to the point much quicker and without taking too much of the customer's time. The Challenger is the ultimate transactional sales consultant.

"I learned that time and money were my real competitors. When I was in front of that customer, I was going to get everything they had to spend on the products I had."

The other four types of salespeople have a tendency to become customer service support people and want to show the customer how helpful they are by being accommodating to everything they think the customer needs before and after the sale is made. You must be the professional during the sales process and then let customer service and support do the after-the-sales professional follow-ups. You can't be revenue producers and customer service professionals at the same time. Use your time producing more sales.

One of the misconceptions of selling is to try and build a relationship with the customer *before* you begin the marketing and sales process. Since the large majority of salespeople have not been trained or well trained, they try to build a *friendship-relationship* with prospects and customers. In reality a relationship in most industries is best built over a number of transactions. This translates to revenue for the customer which begins to build a solid business relationship.

Rather than talking about non-business-related subjects, concentrate on learning about your customers' business and how you can help them achieve their business goals.

When you are helpful and *credible*, the customer makes good selections that result in good sales and revenue for him/her and a trusted business relationship with you. Be pleasant, warm and friendly in a *business manner*. Put your "social visiting" at the end of the sales call, not on the front end and still keep it brief. This will be hard for many salespeople to understand and to embrace as a better way to build good business relationships.

Beware of long conversations with customers and prospects even when the customer is friendly and talkative. All they will remember at the end of the conversation is that you took a lot of their time talking. The next time they will be hesitant to take your call or to make an appointment with you. Remember all calls are business calls and should be measured in content, value and *time*.

Many buyers we speak with in some of the industries I've worked in, like gift and home accessories, are the *owners* of their stores and not just buyers like in a chain or department store or a purchasing agent. Therefore, we will learn how to speak with and sell to "owners" and not just category buyers or purchasing agents.

Store owners are busy multitasking people and appreciate directness and organized knowledge. Even buyers that you do have a good business relationship with will appreciate the business at the front end and all pleasantries on the back end of a business meeting. As a sales manager working with salespeople in the field, I have seen many salespeople run out of time or interrupted while visiting and not getting to the business of the call.

Customers are not interested in niceties such as "hello, how are you" when they are busy. The Challenger helps them move quickly through the selection and buying process.

Another mistake many new salespeople make when starting with a new company or taking over from another sales consultant is wanting to spend time introducing themselves. Since the company and the customer already have a business relationship, put the business at the front end and your accolades about yourself on the back end of the call. They already know the company.

> "Remember all calls are business calls and should be measured in content, value and time."

You see, the business relationship has already been established with the company. You will be building your credibility as a company sales professional delivering the services for which the company is already known. Customers are accustomed to having new salespeople call on them. Don't be the common sales consultant who wants to build a personal relationship before you prove yourself as good or better than the last sales consultant. The Challenger sales consultant can take a customer away from the competition because of their efficient use of knowledge and time.

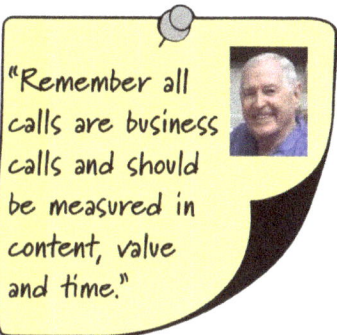

Bunch's Tips
To Success:

1. It's all about the transactions taking place on the sales call.

2. You will be building your credibility as a company sales professional delivering the services for which the company is already known.

3. Be the professional during the sales process and then let customer service and support do the after-the-sales professional follow-ups.

4. I have seen many salespeople run out of time or be interrupted before they conclude their business.

The Fundamentals Of Telephone Sales

Here's my definition of telephone sales and sales in general: *"The daily generation of revenue through constant contact with customers and prospects over the phone or in person."*

Each telephone sales consultant can have around 1,500 customers who are active, inactive or prospective. Of this number, each can have around 600 customers who have bought in the last 18 months. This works because of the call completion rate of 20%-30% of calling 70-80 customers and prospects a day.

Effective use of the telephone is the recommended communication process for today's most efficient and effective method of getting the most sales in the least amount of time. The telephone precedes and follows the other methods. That's why good telephone skills are applicable to all salespeople.

A company's database is one of its most valuable assets and must be worked on and updated constantly. The majority of companies that I have consulted with say that inactive customers are out of business. They are dumbfounded when they sit in on calls and hear the inactive customer say, "Oh, I haven't had anyone call on me from your company in years. Yes, I would love to review your products again."

I am a firm believer in customer retention. I believe that you retain customers by growing their business with you. You should be able to re-activate inactive customers through your calling. I have had the experience with many companies of reactivating several thousand customers back to ordering.

If you are required to work eight hours a day and a big part of your

27

income is derived from earned commissions, you should use those eight hours to be productive talking to customers and researching your customer's history. You can stay later than five o'clock to make calls and send follow-up emails as well as the administrative part of the job or do research for the next day's work. You can even work after dinner at home, but this is up to you.

You are managing your territory, dollars, tasks and accounts. They add up to sales and commissions. Be careful not to let big sales cloud your requirement to work all customers in your territory, or a good sales manager will/should cut your territory. A customer's sales history does not necessarily indicate their size or purchasing power.

You need to be working on a sales historical report (more on this in the next section) that gives you a three-to-four-year history of the customers' buying habits. Many times, these reports show erratic buying because of the lack of attention customers have had from the company and reps. In short, many customers have been left on their own to evaluate their success in selling and buying your company's products/services.

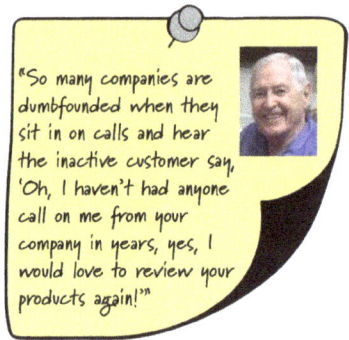

> "So many companies are dumbfounded when they sit in on calls and hear the inactive customer say, 'Oh, I haven't had anyone call on me from your company in years, yes, I would love to review your products again!'"

Customers usually remember your products when they walk by your showroom at trade shows or if they pay attention to your emails or marketing or if they have purchased large enough orders to make your company a valuable resource for them to seek you out. Don't expect their loyalty to continue without your constant and professional attention.

You'll be amazed what you'll find out by your constant attention to your customers:

- That your smaller customers, especially in some fields such as the gift and home accessory industry, do not approach their business on a professional buyer-owner level.

- That your customers are *very receptive* to your calls and help *when you use your new skills* and techniques correctly. This will take practice and discipline to stick with the process.

You should contact your customers four to six times a year as a general rule, and this does not include seeing them at an industry show. Your customers may attend two or more trade shows a year. During peak selling periods like holidays and with seasonal stores, you can call them once every two weeks and collect orders and reorders. If it's a retail account, the weekend changes their needs based on their sales over that weekend. This call is a quick "Hello, <u>what</u> stock do you need to fill in?" *Reminder, it is not "hello, how are you" since how they are is not the purpose of your call.*

We never use the vacuous term "just calling to check on you" or "to see <u>if</u> you needed anything." It is ALWAYS "what do you need." "What" is a think action-question.

You will accomplish much and will move to "expert level" as you continue to learn, experience and *practice, practice and practice* the process you will be learning. Before you begin every sales call, you will review and use the process, applying the following:

- **Planning and creating scripts before making a call, any call.**

- **Scheduling presentations that you have planned out, what you want the buyer to do and when.**

- **Practice and then make the presentation to the customer(s).**

- **Reviewing each call to learn what parts you would keep and what you would change. This also helps develop great listening skills. Listening to yourself and the customer.**

You may trip over and discover sales while practicing this process. The *purpose* is to practice making calls using the new skills and techniques you will be learning. You will begin to make more sales on purpose. You will learn *how and why the process will work for you.* A good way to practice is calling inactive customers.

Bunch's Tips
To Success:

1. Don't expect a customer's loyalty to continue without your constant attention.
2. A customer's sales history does not necessarily indicate their size or purchasing power.
3. A call to a customer should never start with "Hello, how are you," since how they are is not the purpose of your call.

Chapter 4

The Telltale Benchmarks Of Tele Sales

As we're focusing on telephone sales here, let's look at the five benchmarks to being a successful telephone sales consultant:

1. Number of calls dialed.
2. Number of completed calls.
3. Number of presentations scheduled.
4. Number of sales made.
5. Amount of each sale made.

1. Number of calls dialed: This simply means the number of attempts you make to get the buyer or decision maker on the phone. Many times, you will have to make many attempts to get the buyer since they are busy or out of the store or office. On average, you will dial 70 to 80 calls a day. Until you build a relationship through transactions, it is not recommended to leave word on a voice mail or with an associate since they may not know you or your company.

If you get a busy signal, hang up and call the customer back in about 15 minutes. If there is no answer a second time and you get voice mail, then leave a short message that you are attempting to reach them with some information and that you will email or text them and try to reach them again by phone. Long voice mails are not listened to so don't make sales pitches on voice mails or in emails. It is a good idea to script a well written, brief voice mail message.

2. Number of completed calls: The number of completed calls is the number of calls wherein you talked to the buyers you are trying to reach. It is best to arrange as many customers as possible who are similar and require the same message into groups, and then personalize the call to the buyer you are calling. Continue calling until you get the buyer of the company on the phone so you can deliver your message or presentation. On average, you will complete 25% of 70 dialed calls or about 18 "talked-to-the-buyer calls." This can vary from industry to industry.

3. Number of presentations scheduled: The more presentations you schedule the higher the probability of making presentations. You will learn how to confirm the appointment so that the customer keeps the appointment. We are scheduling presentations where we will use our website through screen share. This way we are working just like a rep calling on them in their store except that we are doing it virtually. If you are a road rep, you are scheduling in-person presentations and getting to the point is to your advantage.

4. Number of sales speaks for itself: It is the number of sales you close for the day. That is the goal. The more sales you make, the more dollars you earn for the company and for yourself and the more you help your customers take one more issue off their plate.

5. Amount of each sale: This will determine total dollars for the day. You will learn how to build the sale to larger dollars or add on other categories of products to increase the sale.

When to send emails and texts:

Communication has evolved from the Pony Express, to mail by train, telegraph, telephone, fax, FedEx, email and now to texting and messengering.

Emails have become overused and less read by customers even when they say, "just send me an email." As one customer replied when asked, "Did you get my email?" "Oh, dear, which of the 920 emails I have is yours?" So, here are several effective uses of email:

- Emails for confirmation of appointments and reaffirming the program and your information after the sales call.

- Emails after repeated tries to introduce a new in-house sales specialist program and yourself.

- Emails for markets, special opportunities and events they should know about.

- Emails when customers request specific information.

- Emails to reaffirm and remind customers of what you have shared with them.

Texting is also becoming overused but is still looked at before emails. Use it for important must-know information and, like a good email, keep it short. That is why it is called *texting*. You can text to notify them that you have sent an important email that needs their attention

.

Bunch's Tips To Success:

1. Plan on making 70 to 80 calls a day.

2. On average, you will complete 25% of those dialed calls or about 18 talked-to-the-buyer calls.

3. Emails have become overused and less read by customers even when they say, "just send me an email."

4. Texts should be short, that's why they call them texts.

Chapter 5

Reverse Engineering The Sales Process

One way to look at effective selling is using a reverse engineered formula for reaching desired sales standards and goals. Start at the bottom with what you need to accomplish for the week and month to get to your standard or goal. For the record I believe in attainable standards that you reach daily, weekly and monthly. *Goals are what you personally wish to obtain while standards are what you must achieve.* Start at the bottom of the chart.

Benchmarks for reaching standards and goals:
#Calls, #Completed Calls, #Presentations, Sales and Amount of each Sale, #Emails

Sales Process Funnel

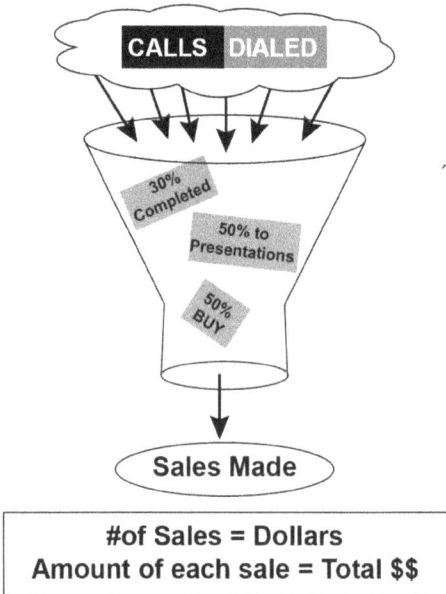

CALLS DIALED

30% Completed

50% to Presentations

50% BUY

Sales Made

#of Sales = Dollars
Amount of each sale = Total $$

Reverse engineer the funnel

7- 70 dialed calls a day

6- 24 completed calls

5- 10 presentations

4 -5 sales

3 -$800 per sales per day = $4,000

2- $20,000 a week (4.5 weeks)

1 monthly $90,000.00

Yearly $1,080,000.00 (start here and read up)

There are 480 minutes (8 hours) in a day: I recommend setting up your day into *three-hour* and *four-hour* time/task slots. Three hours of focused phone calls with no interruptions. You can do these one hour at a time or three hours of calling. Each hour is about 25 dialed calls. Then the other four hours of your day are for other tasks such as your emails, texting, research and planning your 70 calls for the next day.

Activities Score Card for Making Daily/Weekly Sales:

Codes: # dialed calls (DC), # talked with buyer (TW), # left word (LW), # voice mails dialed (VM), # sales (SL),

 # Call back (CB), # no answer (NA), disconnects/out of business (OB), Emailed (EM) Time start/stop

Monday (3 hours calling) 08/ 07/23. Time 9am/10am Time 10am/11am Time 11am/Noon.

DC: _____

TW:_____LW_____VM: _____

SL: _____CB: _____N A: _____OB: _____

Total dials ____ **Total talked** ___ **Send emails**___ **SLS** _____

Tuesday (3 hours calling) 08/ 07/23. Time 9am/10am Time 10am/11am Time 11am/Noon.

DC: _____

TW:_____LW_____VM: _____

SL: _____CB: _____N A: _____OB: _____

Total dials ____ **Total talked** ___ **Send emails**___ **SLS**

Wednesday (3 hours calling) 08/ 07/23. Time 9am/10am Time 10am/11am Time 11am/Noon.

DC: _____

TW:_____LW_____VM: _____

SL: _____CB: _____N A: _____OB: _____

Total dials ____ **Total talked** ___ **Send emails**___ **SLS** _____

Thursday (3 hours calling) 08/ 07/23. Time 9am/10am Time 10am/11am Time 11am/Noon.

DC: _____

TW:_____LW_____VM: _____

SL: _____CB: _____N A: _____OB: _____

Total dials ____ **Total talked** ___ **Send emails**___ **SLS** _____

Friday (3 hours calling) 08/ 07/23. Time 9am/10am Time 10am/11am Time 11am/Noon.

DC: _____

TW:_____LW_____VM: _____

SL: _____CB: _____N A: _____OB: _____

Total dials ____ **Total talked** ___ **Send emails**___ **SLS** ____
Total called for week_____ **Total talked with:** _____
Total number of sales: _____**Total emails sent**_____

I highly recommend not mixing sales calls with other tasks. Rather than time management I call this "task management." The definition of multitasking is doing several things poorly. Selling is kind of like accounting: you cannot do figures and answer the phone, do emails and balance the books at the same time.

Many seasoned salespeople feel they can flip back and forth from task to task and still make meaningful effective sales calls. It is proven that when you switch from writing an email to making a phone call, your mind lingers on the email: Is that what I wanted to say? Was the email well laid out and did I get my point across? Will they read my email?

Do your 3/4 time/task slots and stay on the focused task. You will make great calls and then you will write great emails. Don't flip-flop. The customer will hear the disorganization in your calls and not see the real intent of your emails and texts. All tasks take thought and focus.

It is a lot like production work in a factory. In the textile mills in the 60's and 70's people worked for minimum wages and earned five to ten cents per finished piece. A well-disciplined worker would earn up to an extra $100 a week by focusing on his/her work. Another worker sitting next to her that was unfocused and visiting would only earn an extra $20. Good discipline and focus win every time.

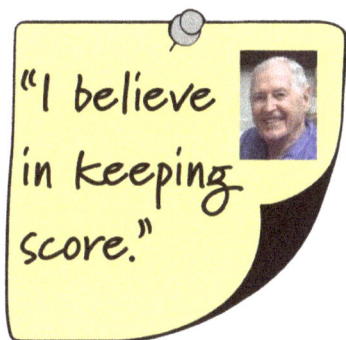

"I believe in keeping score."

If your day is busy writing sales during your three-hour calling time and you do not finish your 70 calls, then use some of the four-hour task time to quickly dial the remaining number of calls.

I believe in keeping my score. Here is a recommended score card. You can change the coding to suit your needs. I recommend making a mark for each result. Four lines and then mark through for five calls, talk with, or call backs etc. This lets you know where you are and what you have accomplished during your calling time.

Bunch's Tips
To Success:

1. Set attainable goals by also having set standards.
2. Work backward from those goals to specifically define the steps necessary.
3. Don't mix calls and emails, you end up doing both less effectively.

Chapter 6

History Counts

A good historical report identifies many things and is a valuable tool. I like to have at least a four-year running report of all my accounts both active and inactive. A good report "talks to you":

1 It shows the history of all accounts. It shows that some customers have only ordered at markets; that some customers reorder between markets; *that when a customer misses seeing us at market, we miss getting his/her order.*

2 It shows that some customers manage their business very well and, without prompting, they order several times a year. It shows the very important "pattern" of good buyers, and the poor pattern of uninformed, unprofessional owners/ buyers we have not contacted. *(Relying on email to do your selling is poor account management.)*

3. One of the most important things you learn from this report is the tremendous opportunity you and the company have with the majority of customers in your territory. It shows customers that you call order and customers that you do not call order only occasionally—if at all—between markets. The term "turns" means how many times a product sells between markets. **Missing a turn is missing sales**.

4. The surprising thing is the lack of consistent orders that result in lower yearly dollars. These numbers occur because buyers inconsistently see you at markets and the lack of attention you have given to customers throughout the year. Remember, when a customer looks at what they purchased, and it is a small amount, they put you in the "not important" category.

I have discovered that the more you grow each customer's business with your company, the less time you have to spend with these customers. Since many salespeople are not well trained, they believe they need to spend more time with larger customers. The reason this is not necessarily so is ***that the more a customer purchases from you the more they stay on top of their business from your company***. I have also learned that the more you are in front of larger customers the more they ask you for deals and discounts. They just require your overview and reminders when they fail to order and reorder.

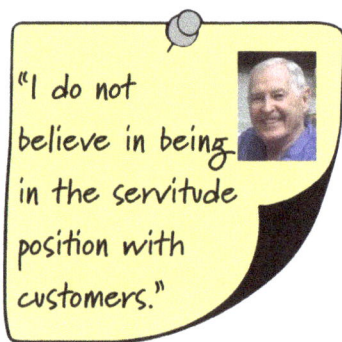

"I do not believe in being in the servitude position with customers."

I learned this while selling to 40 of the top department stores in the Midwest. I kept my professional association with them by not entertaining at New York markets unless I really enjoyed them and had a good business relationship with them. Which means they respected my expertise and credibility because I helped them make their numbers.

I was not their buddy. I only entertained them as a thank you and not as an enticement to get them to buy. I am sure that many will disagree with this but again it is like having a personal relationship with the owner of your company. It is best not to let your owner or customer learn all your shortcomings at a bar or over a long dinner.

A good example of staying away from large customers happened to me with one of my largest stores in Ohio. I received a call that went to my voice mail. I did not get the opportunity to return the call until late afternoon. The buyer said, "Oh, I just needed to cancel $200,000 of orders but have already accomplished that with other vendors." My large orders stayed and were shipped.

A good example of having a good/credible business relationship with customers is the fact that many times I did not show products. A large store simply said to me "Austin, write me up $200K of jewelry and break it out over my A-B-C and D stores."

My customers had the same respect for me, my credibility and time and I returned the respect to them. I do not believe in being in a *servitude* position with customers.

Bunch's Tips To Success:

1. A good historical record of your business with customers is invaluable and should always be employed.

2. Customers that you call order and customers that you do not call order only occasionally — if at all.

3. Letting your customers see you late in the evening after a night of drinking may not be in your best interests.

Part One Summary:

1. Set aside old thoughts and habits to learn a new process to sales.

2. Know your industry, customers and competitors. Some buyers are owners.

3. The job is to become a knowledgeable, organized business professional.

4. Sales redefined: A well-educated sales specialist assisting your customers in having the right products, at the right time, in the right place and at the right price.

5. Learn to become a Challenger sales consultant who challenges the customer.

6. Reverse engineer the selling process to better organize your workflow.

8. The value of sales history data: where the customer has been and the potential of where they can grow.

Learning Powerful Techniques To Obtaining The Sale

Chapter 7

Basic Instructions

Learning the difference between marketing and sales and how **they work together.**

We started Part 1 with the thought that the job of a sales consultant is very often misunderstood and almost always much harder than it appears.

Now, we're going to look into why that's so and what a good sales consultant can do to become a better one. It's about learning the difference between sales and marketing, which are often lumped together but are two very different disciplines.

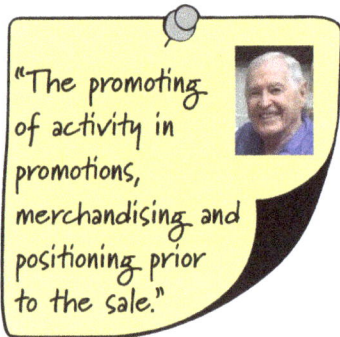

"The promoting of activity in promotions, merchandising and positioning prior to the sale."

But it's much more. It's understanding the core of this training process, knowing the Value Proposition of what you're selling, the discovery element in the selling process and, maybe, most of all, learning perhaps the two most important words of all: "May I."

Let's start with the difference between "marketing" and "sales" ...and there is a big difference that needs to be understood before you make your next sales call. We'll begin the marketing process and move to sales during the training. This is where you will acquire knowledge and experience interacting with the customers and prospects in a non-intrusive manner. This also teaches us the power of communication if we learn the proper way to use it.

Definition of Marketing:

- *"The promoting of activity in promotions, merchandising and positioning prior to the sale."*
- *"The giving and obtaining of information for the purpose of posi-*

tioning the sales process to begin."

- *"The sharing of information about your company and your product that is in line with the customer's needs."*

- *"The gaining of information about the customer so that you understand the customer and the customer's needs."*

- *"Discovery method of learning about the customer and the customer learning about us."*

Marketing   Sales
1. Identify need   2. Close Lead

The common factor in all these definitions is that marketing is identifying the need. Marketing precedes selling.

Definition of Sales:

> *"Transfer of ownership of property from one person (company) to another person (company) in return for money. Sales are the revenue-producing arm of any company. It is how everyone gets paid." [It is how you get paid!]*

Sales is the activity of proceeding to the closed sale. However, our definition of "Sales" is somewhat different:

"The battle of organized knowledge against unorganized knowledge or ignorance."

Broken down, this means that you, the sales consultant, should always be knowledgeable of your products and how your company executes the sales. You must be knowledgeable of your industry and your competitors. You must

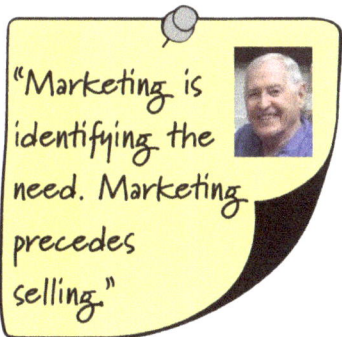

"Marketing is identifying the need. Marketing precedes selling."

be knowledgeable of your marketplace and the customers you are dealing with at any given time. *This knowledge is acquired and built over time.*

Remember that your customers are also salespeople. They buy things to sell. Sometimes store owners forget this fact. You are helping them think proactively in order to make good buying decisions. This is where the word *"helper"* should be substituted for the word *"sales consultant."*

You will be dealing with stores and buyers who are in the business of buying, using and selling products that you and others provide. Your customers purchase products on a daily or weekly basis from someone. You will learn how to present your Value Proposition better than anyone else so that it is easier for the customer to choose your products over any other company.

It is really that simple.

The sales specialists will be learning how to blend marketing and sales into every phone call and sales situation. We use this process each time that we contact the customer in order to learn such things as: who they are, type of store or business and who their customers are and what their interests and needs are at this specific time. This process allows us to transition into the sales process in a natural, non-threatening manner. *It also builds credibility and trust.*

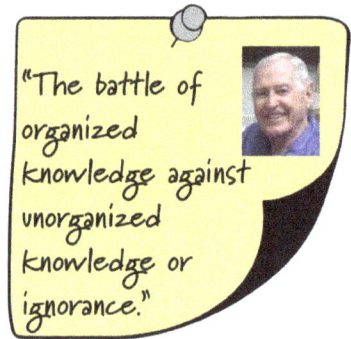

> "The battle of organized knowledge against unorganized knowledge or ignorance."

Bunch's Tips
To Success:

1. There is a difference between marketing and sales. A big difference.
2. Remember that your customers are often salespeople themselves.
3. If you understand the selling process, it's really that simple.

Chapter 8

The Three P's

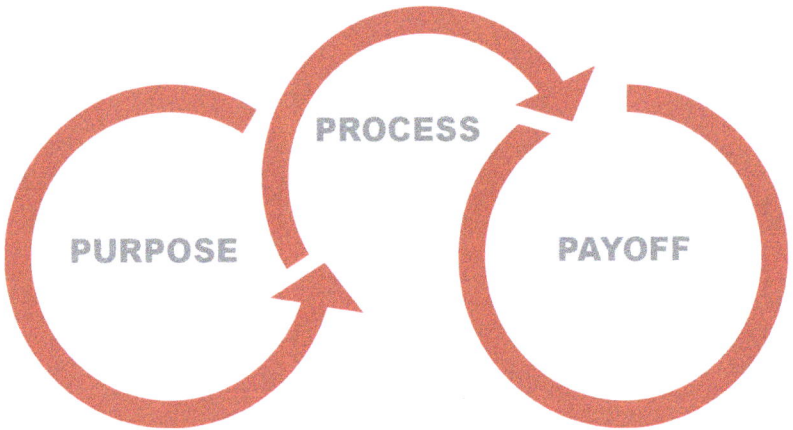

PROCESS

PURPOSE

PAYOFF

T he foundation of all of the training in this program is built around The Three P's model. They stand for: *Purpose, Process and Payoff*.

All of your meetings, phone calls and training follow this format. This formula is a road map to keeping us on track in accomplishing our purpose in an organized and professional manner. This process is designed for transactional and relationship selling.

Before each meeting or phone call, write down the purpose of your call, what process you will follow and what outcome (payoff) you wish to accomplish. At the beginning of every phone call you say, *"the purpose of my call is"* and then follow the process outlined to accomplish your purpose.

Once you have stated your purpose with a customer, you can then share what you want him/her to do, which becomes your desired payoff of the call. In a meeting you share your Purpose, Process and Payoff. This becomes your agenda.

A well-presented agenda in a meeting lets everyone know the purpose of the meeting and how the meeting will flow. The same holds true for a sales call or a well-thought-out sales presentation. It makes everything transparent to the attendees or a customer. Stating the purpose or agenda up front builds trust and shows there is no "hidden agenda."

Understanding Your Purpose Through Self-Coaching

In evaluating yourself you should follow up after each meeting and phone call by asking yourself:

1. *"Did I accomplish my purpose?"*

Did the person I called do what I wanted them to do?

2. *"If I had that call to make over again, what, if anything, would I change? What did I learn from the call?"*

If the answer is "I would change nothing," then keep doing it that way until something changes or until you fail to reach your objective. If there are things you would change then change them and put the changes to the test by using them in making the next phone call.

If it was a good call, you will experience more good calls. If it was a challenging call, you will have another challenging call. That is why we listen to ourselves and the customer, so we know what we said and the customer's response to what we said. Then we fix it for the next call.

Do this exercise after *every phone call both for business and personal calls*. Make it a habit and second nature to coach and mentor yourself. I find that I am the best manager of me since I have always been solution-minded and desire success in everything I do. I don't like a manager catching me not doing the right things, so I always coach myself.

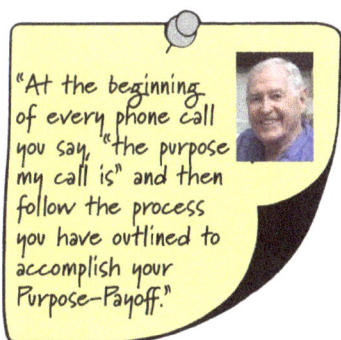

"At the beginning of every phone call you say, "the purpose my call is" and then follow the process you have outlined to accomplish your Purpose–Payoff."

Begin this coaching practice now and practice it after every call you make, business or personal, until it becomes second nature. When you correct the call in your mind, then the corrections become a positive memory of the successful call you intend to make. This correction helps you forget any negative calls and builds confidence and professionalism.

We all carry half-truths and many

51

misconceptions throughout life. My mother always said that parents tell their children "little white lies"—like the storks bring babies—with the intention of correcting them later. Many times, however, we do not get around to correcting the little lies.

I used to do "mini" triathlons where you run, swim and bike. I was very good at running and biking but had a fear of swimming. One day

while practicing my swimming I began to black out in shallow murky water. I stood up and asked myself why did I have this fear? I realize it came from when I was six years old and before I learned how to swim.

I fell into a murky river and was swept downstream where I quickly learned the basics of swimming and got to the bank and safety. I did not drown but I carried the fear of drowning until I realized that I did not drown. I survived. I finished my practice and never had that fear again.

You see, you must fix misconceptions about a lot of things in life and selling is no different. There was a great article in The Wall Street Journal about babies and grownups. The article said that we are born with just two fears: the fear of falling and the fear of loud noises, *all other fears we had to learn.* So as adults we should be throwing off childish things. Even the Bible says, "when I became a man, I put away childish things."

In the book *Mindset*, by Carol S. Dweck, Ph.D., she talks about a fixed Mindset and a growth Mindset. It is a great book about growth, and she writes that we are always a student and must keep learning and doing the things that bring us success. *We are a work in progress and never finished.* I am adding until the Grim Reaper comes for me.

Bunch's Tips To Success:

1. The foundation of selling is built around The Three P's: Purpose, Process and Payoff.
2. The Three P's are used on all phone calls and becomes the agenda.
3. Self-coach yourself after every sales call.

Chapter 9

Knowing The Value Proposition Of The Company And Of Yourself

A Value Proposition is the intangible that sets us apart from the expected or obvious. It is not better products or better prices. It is clear communication, unique and constant service and results beyond expectation.

Different aspects of the selling process have different value propositions:

The definition of a company's Value Proposition:

"When everything appears equal, the value proposition is the monetary worth of importance proposed and delivered to a prospect or customer by a company that sets it apart from other companies. It is what is expected and then much more."

The definition of a sales consultant's Value Proposition:

"When all appearances seem equal, this is the important monetary worth of a sales consultant when working with a customer/prospect that sets them apart from other salespeople. It is the competence and added value you always demonstrate to the customer."

A company's Value Proposition:

What is the company's Value Proposition? What distinguishes the company from all the rest, and what value does the company offer the customers? Some examples of what companies do in an industry like the home accessory and gift field:

---

1. The company designs and researches its products from many countries.
2. The products are researched and designed by a large,

diverse team that provides a leading edge in the market.

3. The company has created several industry-first products and therefore has been copied because of its originality and leadership. Loyal customers stay with the company and are always excited to see what new products it will offer.

4. The company is at the top of the industry in terms of customer satisfaction. It enjoys a reputation for quick response to all customer issues and ascribes to "the customer is always right" practice until a particular customer abuses that generosity.

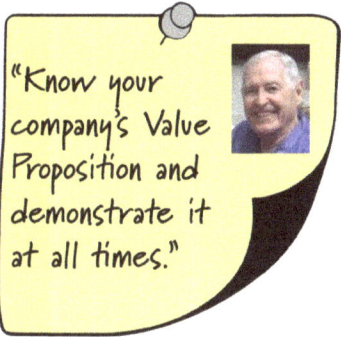

> "Know your company's Value Proposition and demonstrate it at all times."

5. If you build the business on the independent "Mom and Pop" platform, the company must be loyal and committed to this business model. It is difficult to combine other channels such as chain stores and discount stores selling the same products as you are selling the "Mom and Pop" stores.

6. In addition to road reps, the company proudly employs a well-trained in-house sales force of specialists to ensure that its customers have continual service and are well informed on the company's best sellers and industry trends. Because the company collectively talks with hundreds of customers daily across the country, it has the most well-informed salespeople in the industry.

7. The company is an in-stock provider for quick delivery and reordering.

8. It has a fully staffed and well-trained customer service department that quickly responds to its customer's needs.

9. The company has a high standard of practices and quality products and replaces without question.

Create a list of your company's Value Propositions to share with your customers.

In summary, a company's Value Proposition is:

"A supplier of unique products for the moderate and better independent retailers and designers. We consistently execute excellence in products and service above expectations."

The sales consultant's Value Proposition:

This pertains to a company with an in-house sales team or one with its own field salespeople.

1. We are a "one company" specialist. Collectively we speak to over 200 independent stores and designers across the United States every day. (This is true because if you have six or eight telephone salespeople making 70 calls, you are going to talk to 200 customers across the country daily.)

2. We are specialists in our company and knowledgeable of what is happening in the industry in general.

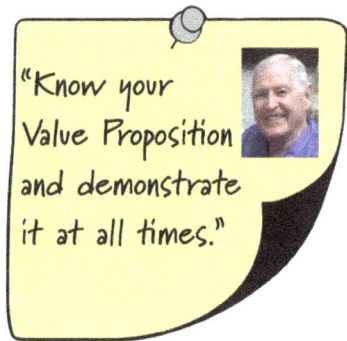

"Know your Value Proposition and demonstrate it at all times."

3. Since we are in-house, we answer all questions quickly and advance your needs and requests without a middle person's interference. You are first on our list of important things to do.

4. We keep you up-to-date and informed on events, sales, specials and trends if you accept our calls and open our emails. We do not send out blind mass emails.

5. Our mission is to keep you well informed and ahead of your competition and share the following with you:

   • What you ordered from our company and how those products are performing across the country.

   • Best sellers and availability.

- Assist you in doing an over-the-phone in-store inventory using your catalogue or your market order sheet with pictures and screen share.

- A conduit of honest and timely information to assist you in making good, informed decisions.

- Work with you offsite using screen share to assist you in selecting the best products, saving you time and reducing stress.

Bunch's Tips To Success:

1. You will become a well-trained specialist on products, industry and your customer's needs.

2. You will be a conduit of honest and timely information to assist the customer in making well-informed decisions.

Chapter 10

Differentiation: How To Be Recognized As The Best

In selling, differentiation is created by the sales consultant as a result of the quality of the presentation of the product line, themselves and the company. We must present everything in a manner that is superior to what is done by any other sales consultant. It is the basis of our Value Proposition.

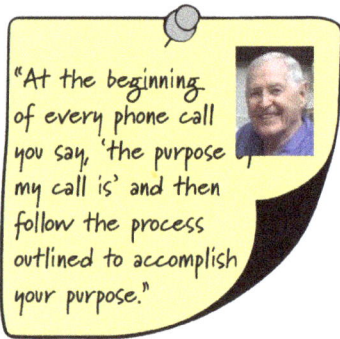

"At the beginning of every phone call you say, 'the purpose of my call is' and then follow the process outlined to accomplish your purpose."

Differentiation can also be used to make it easier and more comfortable for the customer to do business with us. You, the new in-house sales specialist, will be doing several things that relate to the very important revenue-producing component of the company. This department will be working on sales, production and marketing of the company, the team and your products.

Here is where my personal philosophy of selling is very different from many sales managers. **I do not believe that you can mix sales and customer service issues together**. Many managers feel that "One call covers all" and that a sales representative takes care of all customer issues after the sale is made. **A sales consultant is all about revenue production and not maintenance.** I am talking about things like damage issues, wrong products shipped, delivery scheduling and *anything that does not have to do with the sale itself*. All after-the-sale issues should belong to a good customer and sales support person or team. If sales are revenue production, then that is what a sales

consultant's time is meant to do: sell and generate revenue. Not sales support. This is my opinion, and it has served me and my teams very well in all types of industries for more than 50 years.

The answer to the customer's question "I have a broken item, can you take care of it for me, is "No, I do not have that ability, but I can transfer you to Customer Service and they will take care of that for you."

I also do not believe that customer service should ever be in the sales role. Customer service should not take an order or accept a cancellation of an order, that is a sales issue. There are only a few exceptions to making a sale, such as if the sales consultant is not available or anyone else in the sales department is not available. Otherwise, this is a hard and fast rule.

Bunch's Tips To Success:

1. Differentiation and unique Value Proposition are critical in helping you make the sale.
2. Good selling and customer service should never be mixed.

Chapter 11

The Discovery Process: One Thing To Avoid And One To Adopt

Discovery is one skill that the average sales consultant does not do well...if at all.

So, please avoid being average and understand these two important approaches, one to *avoid* and one to *adopt*:

1. Assume-A-Side: Something we do Not want to do:

This comes from a great trainer and good friend who is no longer with us. I learned this from her 25 years ago, and it has helped me and hundreds of salespeople not to make ***assumptions*** about anything, let alone about our customers and prospects.

I call it "assume-a-side." This is "the assumption that you know something before you have asked qualifying questions of the customer." Or you assume that the customer knows everything about you and your company.

"Don't assume anything: ask and then listen!"

You will learn not to finish or interrupt a customer or anyone else's sentence because this is rude and assumptive, and many times you will be wrong with your assumption. This makes you lose credibility and respect from the customer, or anyone with whom you are working.

When you ask a customer a question, ***wait/pause*** and ***listen*** to the answer before you speak.

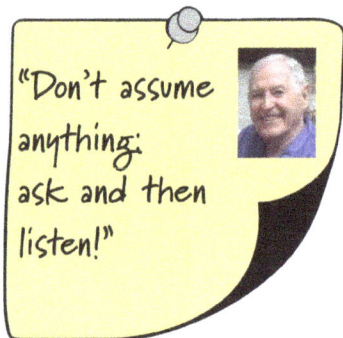

A few examples of assume-a-sides:

1. Assuming a customer does not want to talk to you.

2. Assuming a customer has everything he/she needs so you don't make the call.

3. Assuming the customer wants to end the call because of the way he/she sounds. (A customer will tell you if he/she can't talk.)

4. Assuming a customer will call you when he/she sells out of your best sellers.

5. Assuming you have sold everyone and there is no one else to sell.

6. Assuming your customers are always right and therefore you do not challenge them to rethink their position.

7. Assuming during economically challenging times that no one is buying anything.

"Don't interrupt or finish people's sentences."

8. Assuming that because a customer was short or in a hurry that you should not call him/her again.

9. Assuming that negative notes from the last sales consultant in your company are correct and therefore you do not call that customer.

10. Assuming what they said last week is true this week.

11. Assuming customers always open and read your emails and follow your recommendations.

12. Assuming that if several customers did not answer the phone, you stop making calls.

Here is a great example from one of my good students, Deanie Walker, on an assume-a-side:

"I called a customer who had just ordered so many display units that I assumed they did not need any at this time. In my head I was thinking there is no way they would order more. I made the call and to my pleasant surprise they ordered 52 more units plus other items. An over $30K order that if I had kept my assumption, I wouldn't have gotten that order. This put me at number one for the week."

Don't ever assume, ask-pause and then listen!

2. "May I": A powerful tool in selling you WANT to use:

"May I" is one of the most powerful tools of selling. You will learn to always use the term "May I" when making a discovery or asking any questions. The customer will give you a *road map* of how to sell them if you ask good questions, listen, give verbal right-of-way and do not commit *assume-a-sides*.

Here's the important distinction: "*May I*" is asking permission. "Can I" is asking if you know how. Saying "let me tell you" is rude.

Some examples of using "May I":

- May I ask a little about your store?

- May I share with you some of our best sellers?

- May I show you around the showroom and point out new products?

- May I ask why you chose to visit our showroom?

- May I ask why you feel that way? (Does not like an item, did not do well with a product, and does not think they can sell an item and so on.)

- May I make an appointment with you this week?

- May I ask what questions you have of me? (Rather than, do you have any questions?)

Always use "May I" to clearly understand what the customer's issues are _before_ you attempt to offer a solution.

- "I am going to wait until market to order." May I ask why you want to do that?

- "I have no open to buy now." "May I ask when you expect that to change?"

- "Our sales are down." "May I ask why you think they are at this time?"

- May I ask, "what is doing well for you at this time?"

- May I ask, "what other vendors are doing well for you?"

- May I ask, "why do you feel the product is not performing well?"

- May I call you tomorrow to complete the order?

- May I share a little about myself and my company?

- May I ask what are some major challenges that I may help you with?

"May I" is a great way to keep the conversation going when you are at a loss for words, or you are speaking with a non-responsive person. Example: May I ask you to share a little more with me?

During one training session a few years ago one of my students hung up the phone and shared with the room her experience with a surprised call. The person she was calling was a little stand-offish and almost rude. In response to the "May I" approach, the customer said, "I usually do not take these types of calls, but you were so polite and informative I just had to listen. I am glad I did and yes, I would like to hear more about your products."

"May I' is one of the most powerful tools of selling."

I have many clients whose complete culture has been improved using "May I" and The Three P's in their phone calls, meetings and daily interactions with employees and managers.

Bunch's Tips
To Success:

1. Don't assume you know what your customer is thinking.
2. Asking permission, using "May I" is an amazing sales technique.
3. Listen to your customer...and then listen some more.
4. Combined with The Three P's, using "May I" can change your whole selling culture.

Chapter 12

What To Ask In The Discovery Process

Now that you know how to conduct the Discovery Process – using the "May I" technique and The Three P's – here are some of the things you'll want to know and will discover. This will happen over time but not all at once.

1. All pertinent information about the account such as shipping and mailing address, phone numbers, fax and email, contact person's full name and other important contacts. All this information is a must when setting up a customer account. Always get their full name.

2. Type of store: gift, garden, home accessory, furniture, interior design shop, seasonal or some combination of categories. This becomes important when you are calling a customer/prospect to know what type of products to present and what type of questions to ask.

3. Where the store is located: shopping mall, strip mall or self-standing? This gives you an idea of the amount of traffic they have.

4. How long have they owned the business? Approximate yearly sales? (If they are hesitant, say more or less than $500K-$1M.) How long has the customer been in business will give you an idea how knowledgeable and experienced the customer is in the business. New customers need more hand-holding

"Credibility is hard to earn, easy to lose and very hard to gain back. It is always better to say, I don't know, but if you wait a moment, I will find that out for you.' You will practice this always and forever."

whereas seasoned customers need good information,

reminding them what they've purchased and recommendations.

5. The size of the store: 1000 sq. ft., 2000 sq. ft. or maybe the size of a small home? How many trailer trucks could you park in your store? This gives you a reference for how much they can buy for the store based on space.

6. Do they try to have things in their store that appeal to a high end, moderate, or entry level customer? Do they have a variety of price-layering of products or are more focused on a particular type of customer or price point? Does the store have a particular theme? This knowledge helps you decide what type and price of products to recommend to the customer.

7. What are some of the best-selling categories of products and price points? This gives you an idea of where to concentrate your sales presentation and what products to show and what not to show.

8. What is their process and what prompts them to order between markets? Is it as they sell down an item, results of doing an inventory, keeping best sellers in stock or when a customer asks for items that are out of stock? This lets you know how they really do business and if they are on top of their business.

9. Who are some of their other good vendors? (Let them give company names, then reference companies that are in your type of business and that you compete with.) As you attend markets you will learn more about other vendors. Reading industry magazines and researching a competitor's website is also a good way to learn about other vendors and industry knowledge. This gives you an idea of what their store merchandise looks like.

10. How do they make their purchase? At markets (where and when), from reps, phone in to vendors, Internet, catalogs? What about reordering? This tells you how to do business with them.

11. How do they keep up with what is and is not selling in

their store? Computer readouts, taking a physical inventory by walking around or discovering that they are out when customers ask for a product? Again, this helps you understand how they run their business.

12. Has the store changed over the years in terms of products, customers and other directions, and if so, how? This helps you understand if they are staying current and are proactive to growing.

13. What are some of the things they are doing this year to combat slower than usual sales? What is working? What has worked well in the past? Are they progressive and proactive or are they cautious and conservative.

14. What is the best way to communicate with the store—phone, email, text, fax? How to best contact them and confirm they will respond to your calls—email, text, fax.

15. Are they seasonal or year-round? What is their stronger selling times of the year? This lets you know how often to call them in case they are more of a seasonal store as opposed to an all-year store.

16. How did they first discover your company, and what appealed to them? This lets you know how they shop in general and what appeals to them when at markets.

There is other valuable information to gain from the customer/prospect. It is very surprising how many salespeople make assumptions—assume-a-sides—and do not ask the following questions of every customer, even if they have been calling on them for years.

"It is very surprising how many salespeople make assumptions even if you have been calling on a customer for years."

1. What do they expect and want from a sales consultant?

2. What are things a sales consultant does that irritates them so that you know what not to do.

3. What are the important things we should share with them so, you know what to do.

Knowledge You Want To Gain During the "Conversational" Part of Your Call:

1. Always get information about the customer, whether it is profile information or current information about their weekend sales, changes in the business or what is selling.

2. Information can be gained from the buyer or from store personnel. Getting information from store personnel prepares you for when you do get the buyer on the phone, so that you sound well informed.

3. Are there any changes in direction or additions to the store? Sometimes they have added a second store.

4. Show interest in what they are doing.

5. Information is discussed after the purpose of the call has been covered unless the purpose of the call is to gain information.

One of the best times to gain valuable and updated information about the customer is during markets. This can occur after the business has been concluded, and you should say, "May I ask how the business is doing and what changes have occurred?"

You can also make a marketing call and ask the customer to share a little about his/her business. Keep to marketing and do not switch to selling on these types of calls.

The "I AM NEW" Card

Do not hesitate to play the "I am new" card with the prospect/customer when you are doing your discovery. This will relax the customer

and they will gladly answer your questions. When you are not sure of an answer to a customer's question you can always get the answer from your manager or a coworker.

In the training phase and for the first year with a company you are a new person, and you are not expected to be as knowledgeable as someone with several years of experience with the company.

Never bluff or guess at an answer since you are always building credibility with the customer. When you master this training, you will progress faster than the majority of new salespeople and be ahead of many experienced salespeople who are still using old school sales tools. Follow instructions to success.

We have to realize that a majority of the time we call or see our customers and prospects when they are ignorant or unsure of what our products or services are or what we can do for them. By applying the principles of The Three P's, you will become very good at quickly gaining the customer's or prospect's interest and beginning the marketing/sales process. You will be educating the customer on many things including good industry standards of buying, selling and good merchandising ideas.

Bunch's Tips
To Success:

1. The Discovery Process is invaluable in helping you sell, just don't expect to learn everything at once.
2. Don't be afraid to ask a customer what do they expect and want from a sales consultant?
3. Always get information from the customer. Play the "I am new" card when in fact you are new.
4. One of the best places to get information is at a market or trade show.
5. What have you learned that will help you sell the customer?
6. What do you still not know that will help you sell the customer?

Part Two Summary:

1. Marketing is information gathering and sharing to prepare for the sale. Sales is the transferring of ownership from one company to another.

2. You become a sales specialist through Process, Discovery and Outcome.

3. The foundation of the program is The Three P's: Purpose, Process and Payoff.

4. The value of self-coaching: Why am I calling? Did I accomplish my purpose? If I had the call to do over again, what, if anything, would I say or do differently?

5. Always be organized and knowledgeable to therefore be credible.

6. The Value Propositions: Yours and the company's.

7. The Art of Differentiation: Assume-a-side is something you do not want to commit.

8. Using "May I" is something you do.

9. Think of yourself as a guide.

10. Always gather information about the customer.

Learning How To Be Versatile In Communicating With Others

Chapter 13

The Communications Tool: Social Styles

We all know how to talk – some of us better than others – but real communication is something else entirely. It's why we're going to spend a little time here discussing Social Styles.

Social Styles is a discovery tool that gives a pretty good indication of how a person communicates and how best to communicate with him or her. It is not about personality or the ability to listen. It is about the way we process information and then react to the information we have received.

First off, there are four Social Styles:

1. Analytical

2. Driver

3. Amiable

4. Expressive

We all have some of these traits, but one trait is our dominant style. A very big part of selling is communicating so that the customer becomes comfortable, and we begin to build trust. We know that people are different not only in appearance and personality but in how they receive, process and react to information.

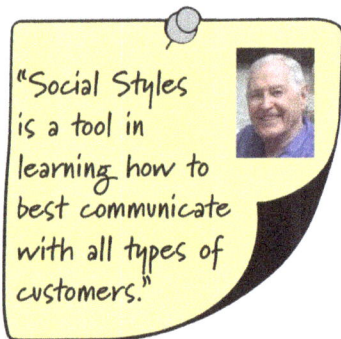

"Social Styles is a tool in learning how to best communicate with all types of customers."

The average sales consultant is not familiar with Social Styles. The sales consultant who has studied Social Styles has a big advantage over other salespeople because this valuable tool teaches how to communicate differently with people based upon their individual Social Style.

That's why we are providing an overview of Social Styles to give you a good working knowledge of what it is and how to use it to your advantage in communicating with the customer. You will have to learn to listen to the customer and pay attention to their pace of speaking and their reactions to your pace and style of speaking in order to determine their communication style. This tool will help you first identify the social style of the customer, and then adjust to the style of the person you are speaking with. This will greatly improve your chances of building trust, give you a better understanding what the other person is saying and move on to the sale. It's not only fun but it can even be used in your everyday experiences to improve relationships and overall communication.

"The average sales consultant is not familiar with Social Styles so the one that has studied them has a big advantage."

The Social Styles Profile

The best way I've seen to understand this is to use the Social Style Profile developed by David Merrill and Roger Reid in their book, *Personal Styles & Effective Performance*, published by Chilton in 1981 and then referenced by Wilson Learning in their 2004 book *Social Styles Handbook*. The model works as a 2X2 matrix, as you'll see in the chart below. The first distinction is mainly between the individual's level of *Assertiveness* and the second distinction is based on *Responsiveness*.

Here's how each is defined:

Assertiveness:

The degree to which people have opinions about issues and make their positions on those issues public.

In other words, it is not that they have strong opinions, but that they frequently express them directly and often attempt to persuade others to their view.

Responsiveness:

This is the degree of emotionalism people display in public situations. Responsive people "wear their emotions on their sleeve," as the saying goes, while less responsive people would tend not to let their emotions show. Responsive people also tend to be casual and informal in social situations.

So, how do you use all of this?

1. Determine your own style:

Review the descriptions of each style and classify yourself. Also ask those you trust for their opinions. Remember you are looking for your "base" style. So, that doesn't mean under certain conditions you won't act in one of the other roles, but it means you are trying to determine the style you most naturally fall into. Once you have identified yourself, you can review the information concerning this style's strengths and weaknesses and factor those into your approach.

2. Adjust your communication approach:

As the sales consultant it is your task to make the adaptive move towards the style of the customer. This is hard but can pay off. It is suggested that you begin interactions by keeping your initial

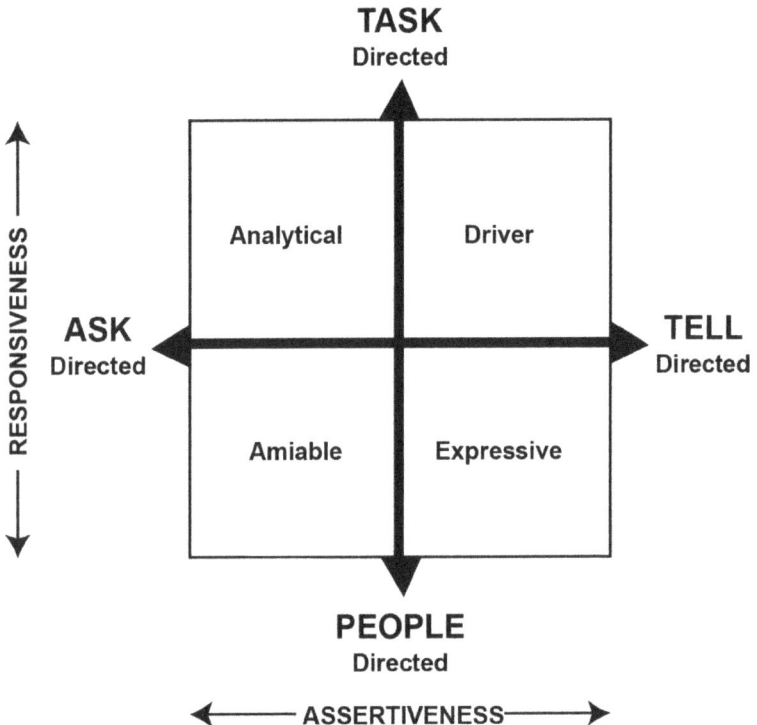

TASK
Directed

Analytical	Driver
Amiable	Expressive

ASK
Directed

TELL
Directed

RESPONSIVENESS

PEOPLE
Directed

ASSERTIVENESS

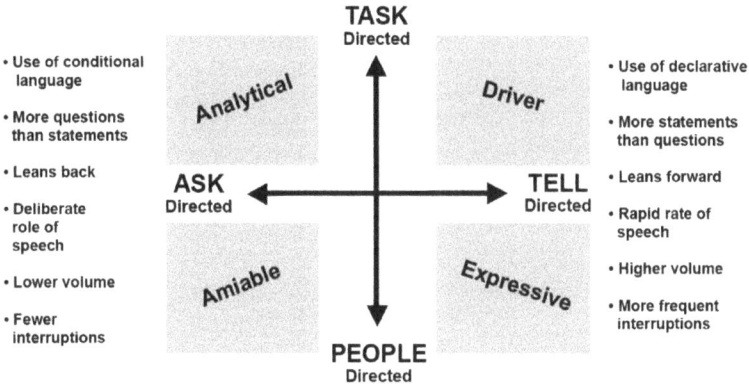

• Fewer gestures minimal body language

• Consistent tone and voice inflection

• Shares and dispays fewer emotions

• Less facial expression

• Dialogue focused first on task and facts

TASK
Directed

• Use of conditional language

• More questions than statements

• Leans back

• Deliberate role of speech

• Lower volume

• Fewer interruptions

Analytical

Driver

ASK
Directed

TELL
Directed

Amiable

Expressive

• Use of declarative language

• More statements than questions

• Leans forward

• Rapid rate of speech

• Higher volume

• More frequent interruptions

PEOPLE
Directed

• More and wider gestures and body language

• Varied tone and voice infection

• Shares and displays more emotions

• More facial expression

• Dialogue focused first on people and relationship

approach right in the middle of the grid (so as not to become an immediate mismatch) and then adjust as you get to know the customer. Speak in middle tones, pace yourself until you determine the customer's style and then try to match his/her pace, tone and style of speaking.

Let's look first at a matrix that takes Assertiveness and Responsiveness and plots them against the four Social Styles:

Once you've reviewed this it's time to dig deeper and look for the Behavior Clues that will tell you the Social Style of your customers and how to communicate with them.

Ok, the final communication tool here is to take this understanding of your customers and truly understand what they want in a business conversation with you.

Analyticals Want...	Drivers Want...
• A more formal and structured approach	• A businesslike attitude with a focus on effective problem solving
• Enough time to think things through	• Efficient use of time
• Evidence of how results were achieved	• Evidence of results
• Clear, logical processes	• Strong product knowledge
• Support for their thinking and principles	• Documentaion and facts
• Data that aids decision making	• Clear benefits
• Respect	• Support for their ideas
	• Options and choices
	• Power

Amiables Want...	Expressives Want...
• A open and honest approach	• More flexible use of time
• Time to develop the relationship with the salesperson	• Discussions that keep movong and stay focused
• Support for feelings	• Others to get to know them as people
• Assurances	• Personal recognition for their ideas and actions
• Other's involvement in the decision making process	• Strong product lmowledge
• Clarity of impact on others	• Not too much detai
• To know why it's right	• Testimonials as evidence of success
• Approval	• Recognition

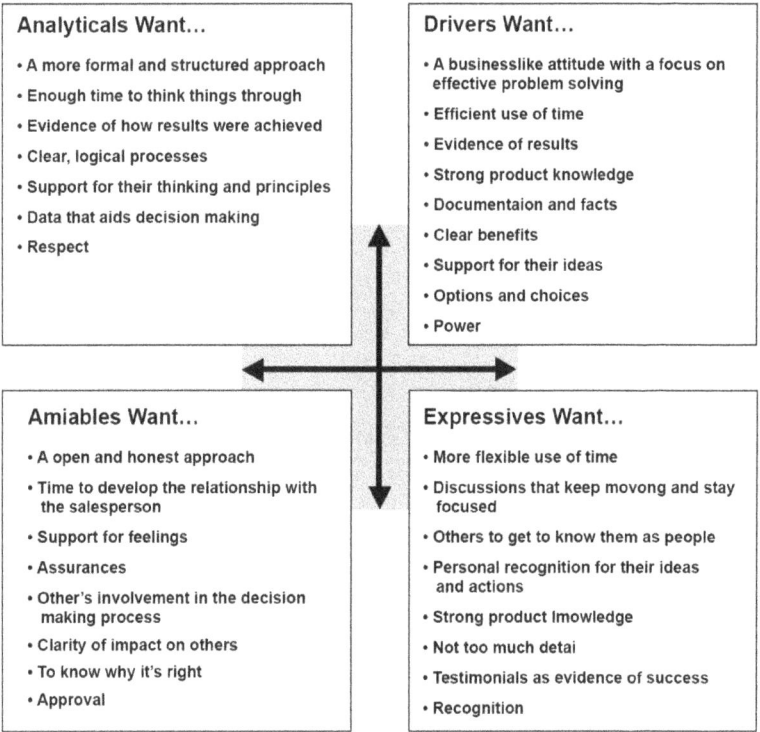

What is YOUR Social Style?

As you identify the Social Style of the person on the other side of this business conversation, it's just as important to understand your Social Style, as communication is a two-way street. By taking this quick quiz, you will get that answer.

A couple of ground rules first. Do not overthink your answers since this is not a test. It's a quick and simple way to give you a pretty good idea of your Social Style and how you interact with people. Of course, this questionnaire is not 100% on the money, but over the years I've found it has proven to be about 70% accurate.

Relax and be objective about yourself, there is no right or wrong answers. Answer the questions as you know you are, not as you would like to be.

Determine which of the four comments most accurately describes you and place a number "4" on that line. Then decide which of the remaining three comments are most like you and then place a number "3" on that line. Rank the remaining two comments by placing the number "2" and the number "1" on the appropriate line, so that "1" is the least like you of all four.

Answer all sections in a like manner and check your answers when you're done to be sure that all statements have the four comments rated from 1 to 4, using each number only once.

And by the way, as I said before, this is not just for business. After you answer the questions and score yourself, give it to a mate or close friend to learn where they scored. It has helped a lot of family members and married couples to better understand each other and improve their misunderstandings of each other.

1. WHEN I AM AT WORK I PREFER TO BE SEEN:

A. ( ) Correct and accurate

B. ( ) Outgoing and enthusiastic

C. ( ) Dependable and reliable

D. ( ) Efficient and quick to get on with the job

2. I PREFER TO WORK WITH PEOPLE WHO ARE:

A. ( ) Self-controlled, able to sort out the facts to get the job done

B. ( ) Fun to be with and are motivating

C. ( ) Supportive of other people, considerate of personal objectives

D. ( ) Independent, able to get on with their work with minimum supervision

3. I FEEL OF MOST VALUE WHEN I CAN:

A. ( ) Work out the details of a new concept or idea at my own pace

B. ( ) Motivate others towards goals that I consider important

C. ( ) Show others how to practically apply a new idea or concept

D. ( ) Get others to expand themselves

4. WHEN PEOPLE UPSET ME I FEEL LIKE:

A. ( ) Avoiding them and getting on with other things that are important to me

B. ( ) Telling them how I feel about the situation in no uncertain manner

C. ( ) Agreeing with them to avoid the personal conflict

D. ( ) Confronting them and telling them what is wrong

5. I PREFER TO LEAD PEOPLE BY:

A. ( ) Consulting with them to ensure that they stay on track

B. ( ) Creating open, active discussions to build personal motivation

C. ( ) Sharing how I feel about the situation to gain their support

D. ( ) Directing them toward the achievement of the job at hand

6. I LIKE OTHERS TO SEE ME AS A PERSON WHO:

A. ( ) Is disciplined and thorough in everything that I do

B. ( ) Enjoys social interaction and companionship

C. ( ) Understands other people well enough not to cause personal conflict

D. ( ) Is tough and demanding but always fair

7. WHEN I HAVE AN IMPORTANT DECISION TO MAKE, I LIKE TO CONSIDER:

A. ( ) The facts that I personally have found to be correct

B. ( ) Recommendations made by people I respect

C. ( ) The opinions and feelings of the people closest to me

D. ( ) The various options available to arrive at the best alternative

8. WHEN I AM ASKED TO HELP ANOTHER PERSON, I LIKE TO:

A. ( ) Take my time to observe what their situation is and then discuss what can be done

B. ( ) Confront them as quickly as possible to help them get back on track

C. ( ) Be supportive of their situation so that I understand how they feel

D. ( ) Discover what their problem is and then tell them what they need to do

9. CLOSE FRIENDS WOULD MOST LIKELY DESCRIBE ME AS:

A. ( ) Reliable, dependable and well organized

B. ( ) A fun loving person who has a good personality

C. ( ) Trustworthy and a good friend to have when in need

D. ( ) Opinionated and headstrong, but often right

10. WHEN I MEET PEOPLE FOR THE FIRST TIME, I PREFER TO:

A. ( ) Be careful to project a favorable appearance

B. ( ) Be sociable and friendly to relax them and get to know them quickly

C. ( ) Be friendly, but take time to establish a relationship

D. ( ) Be myself, whether they like me or not

11. WHEN I AM UNDER EMOTIONAL STRESS:

A. ( ) I like to withdraw to avoid the people causing me the stress

B. ( ) I sometimes do hurtful things that I regret later

C. ( ) I become personally hurt by the thoughtless actions of other people

D. ( ) I am easy to anger

12. WHEN WORKING WITH OTHER PEOPLE, I LIKE TO BE:

A. ( ) Accurate and well organized

B. ( ) Creative and involved in a variety of activities

C. ( ) Friendly and part of the team

D. ( ) In charge (and/or) actively involved in getting the job done

13. WHEN SOCIALIZING, I PREFER TO:

A. ( ) Have a quiet formal dinner party with close acquaintances

B. ( ) Enjoy a fast paced party with a variety of people

C. ( ) Have a relaxed, informal, casual get together

D. ( ) Be private, sharing my best with only one other

14. WHEN IN A CLOSE RELATIONSHIP WITH ANOTHER PERSON, I PREFER TO:

A. ( ) Be discrete and proper, not openly demonstrating my feelings in front of others

B. ( ) Show my affection openly, enjoying close contact

C. ( ) Enjoy a close, gentle association demonstrating warmth

D. ( ) Take it or leave it, as I consider it is not necessary to continually give or receive affection to prove it exists

15. WHEN COMMUNICATING WITH OTHER PEOPLE, I PREFER TO:

A. ( )Take my time, asking them what they think about the matter

B. ( ) Be open and prepared to negotiate to achieve my objectives

C. ( ) Be tactful and sensitive to their feelings about the situation

D. ( ) Get to the point and tell them how I see the situation

NOW THAT YOU HAVE COMPLETED THE PROJECT, PLEASE TOTAL THE NUMBERS IN THE PARENTHESES AS FOLLOWS:

1. Total of the "A" (___)   3. Total of the "C" (___)

2. Total of the "B" (___)   4. Total of the "D" (___)

TOTAL (   )

There are 15 questions and therefore 15 A, B, C and D's. You are adding all of the numbers that you put in the 15 A's, then 15 B's, then 15 C's and then 15 D's. Your total will be 150.

Now take the total of "A" which is number one and put that number on the score chart. Then do the same with "B" which is number two, then "C" which is number three and then "D" which is number four.

Then draw a triangle that connects the numbers. That will show you a person's natural comfort zones. When you add up "A" and "C," which is on the left side, that number should not be much above 74-78 for a good sales consultant. When you add up "B" and "D," that number should be between 72 and 78.

It is very hard to find these numbers for a good balanced assertive sales consultant, but you should get as close as you can. On the other hand, if you accept a nice friendly person who has a score of 80 to 85 of A & B, you will struggle to get them to be assertive in the sales role. They are great at customer service but not in sales that requires selling volume to all types of customers.

Some other contributing factors of good candidates are age—the longer we live the more we learn to adjust, past experiences, past training and good management.

No exercise like this is foolproof but by understanding your own Social Style and that of the people you will be doing business with you have a much better chance of being successful as a sales consultant. The numbers may not tell the whole truth, but they also don't lie.

Communication Style
Based on your response to our questionaire this profile reflects your current combination of traits

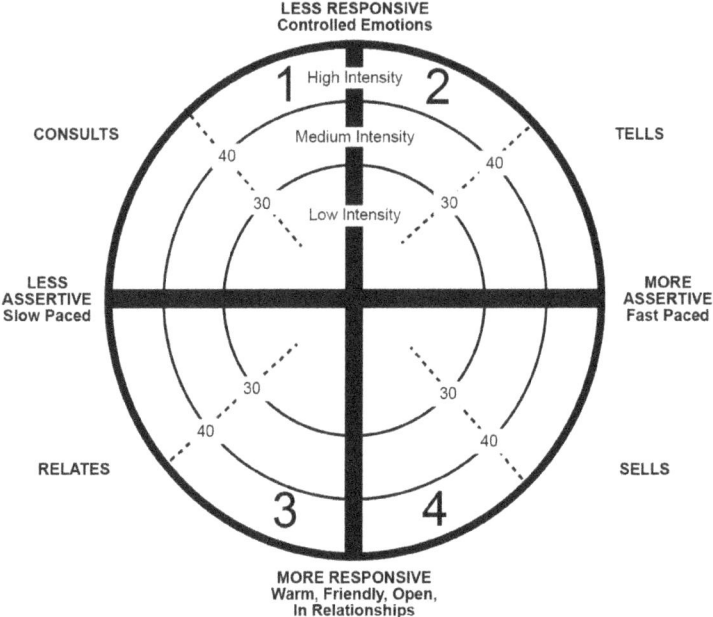

LESS RESPONSIVE
Controlled Emotions

High Intensity

1   2

CONSULTS   TELLS

Medium Intensity

40   40

30   Low Intensity   30

LESS ASSERTIVE
Slow Paced

MORE ASSERTIVE
Fast Paced

30   30

40   40

RELATES   SELLS

3   4

MORE RESPONSIVE
Warm, Friendly, Open,
In Relationships

Bunch's Tips
To Success:

1. There are four Social Styles: Analytical, Driver, Amiable and Expressive.

2. When it comes to Social Styles, you have either Assertiveness or Responsiveness.

3. Start off your interaction with a customer in neutral territory until you find out his/her Social Style.

4. Understanding your own Social Style can be even more important than knowing your customers'.

Part Three Summary:

1. Social Styles is a tool for learning how to best communicate with all types of customer communication styles.

2. There are four profiles of communication: Analytical, Driver, Amiable and Expressive.

3. Adaptability means adjusting your style of communication to the customer's.

4. Assertiveness is the degree to which people express opinions about issues in public.

5. Responsiveness is the degree of emotionalism people display in public situations.

6. Learn and look for behavior clues to identify Social Styles.

7. Understand preferences and expectations as a guide to how to interact with each Social Style.

Part Four

It's All About
The Script

Chapter 14

The Amazing Telephone

In many industries, companies' salespeople present products to the marketplace in four ways:

1. Through industry magazine advertisements.

2. At industry trade shows and markets where you can see customers and show products.

3. Through direct reps and independent reps calling on stores in the field.

4. On the phone, through well trained, in-house salespeople using their website, screen shares, texting and emails.

When using the telephone, scripting is a most valuable tool. We use scripts to make appointments, make sales on the phone with accounts that a rep missed seeing on the road and by customer service people. A good script also applies when a prospect calls for information.

Scripts can be used with numbers 3 and 4 of the above types of selling activities but right now we're going to focus on number 4, using the phone to make sales directly to the customers.

In fields like the home accessory, gift and apparel industries, where I've spent extensive time, as well as in many other industries, 80% of customers see our products at one of the markets or trade shows, through advertising or in other stores. We then use the telephone to contact the customer to assist, direct and make recommendations and conclude the sale in an efficient manner. We do this using screen share apps like Join-Me and Zoom as well as newer technologies.

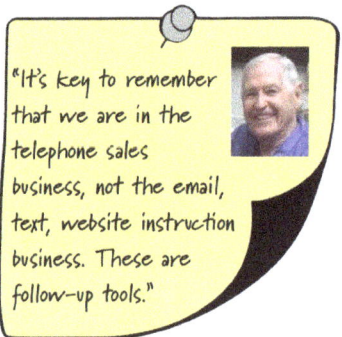

"It's key to remember that we are in the telephone sales business, not the email, text, website instruction business. These are follow-up tools."

The advantages of using the phone over calling on customers in person:

A rep calling on a customer in his/her store does not carry many, if any, samples but works from a set of catalogues or a laptop just like we use by screen share while on the phone with the customer.

The rep calling on the customer in the store takes up anywhere from

30 minutes to several hours of the customer's time during the sales call. We accomplish more dollars in about 20 minutes (and sometimes more dollars in even less time) over the phone. Plus, the road rep is limited in the number of customers he/she can call on in one day. Effective use of the phone enables us to call on many more customers in a day and to make more sales.

It's key to remember that we are in the telephone sales business and not the email, text or website instruction business. Emails, texts and websites are last resorts for giving good instruction and follow-up tools. We want customers to come to us so that we can guide and direct them over the telephone by using screen share to produce solutions and for best selections of our products.

A large majority of our competitors' sales forces are poorly, if at all, trained and therefore bring very little value to the customers. Many customers are very selective when working with salespeople. This is why you will learn to always bring not only value but added value to your customers.

Bunch's Tips
To Success:

1. Scripting can be used in four types of selling activities.

2. Effective use of the phone enables us to call on many more customers in a day and to make more sales.

3. A large majority of our competitors' sales forces are poorly, if at all, trained and therefore bring very little value to the customers.

Chapter 15

Here's Why Scripts Are So Important

Why use Scripts?

There are many reasons why using a script is so important for the selling process. Let's start with a very important one:

A practiced script makes my voice intonation, speaking style and flow sound professional. It also helps me sound competent. Scripts will make you better at selling over the phone. They will make you sound more professional and knowledgeable. Scripts have the added benefit of freeing your mind to focus on your message and your audience rather than on the words you use.

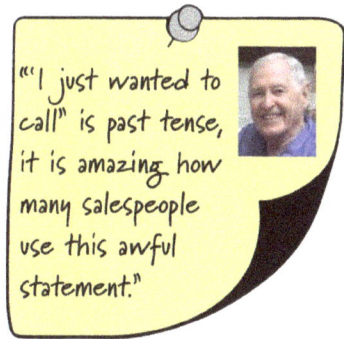

> "'I just wanted to call" is past tense, it is amazing how many salespeople use this awful statement."

And scripts work so well in sales because there are so many repetitive activities: making cold calls, setting appointments, making follow-up calls, giving elevator speeches, offering product demos, answering questions, making presentations, overcoming objections and making closes.

Scripts also take the fluff and distracting "fillers" out of the calls. Things like, "oh yes, that's great," "oh, I know what you mean," "fabulous," "yeah-yeah" and many other replies that are not necessary and are *distracting* on the phone to the customer and can affect your ability to intently listen.

When you have a script, you never have to worry about what to say or not to say. A script also helps you say what is important on every call. Every phone call is an interruption, even if a family member is calling. You have about 10 to 15 seconds to answer three questions in the customer's mind.

1. "Who is calling me?"

2. "Why are they calling me?"

3. "What value is it to me to stop what I am doing and engage in this call?"

We all use scripts whether we realize it or not. If you recorded yourself making five sales calls in a day you would hear yourself saying the same things, just in a random, disorganized manner. We repeat what the customer *wants* to hear rather than planning out what the customer *needs* to hear.

Whether you are making phone calls or calling on customers in person, both create stress and tension. We find ourselves reacting to or defensive to what the customer is saying rather than presenting our ideas/agenda in a prepared and professional manner.

"One of the important tools of selling is a good descriptive vocabulary."

Choosing the right words and phrases to put into our scripts.

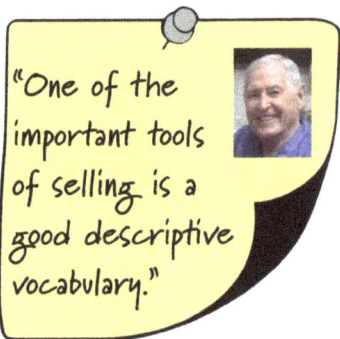

The right words are your friends. There are strong directive words and there are passive words. One *of the important tools of selling is a good descriptive vocabulary.* Developing your sales and communication vocabulary is a constant task. You can learn by listening to talk show hosts, newscasters, podcasts and by reading. Not only does a good command of descriptive words and phrases make you a better communicator, it also quickly *differentiates* you from the masses. Substituting uncommon words for commonly used words helps keep your customer's attention.

Here are some great examples of how to improve often used phrases:

- *"We are having a great opportunity buy"* rather than "we are having a sale."

- *"I am calling to recommend you take advantage of the limited quantities of a great new product"* rather than "I don't want you to miss out."

- *"Here are a few of our most purchased and reorder items"* rather than "here are our best sellers."

- *"The purpose of my call"* rather than "I am calling because" or "the reason I am calling" or "just calling to check on you."

- *"The purpose of my call is to share some exciting news"* rather than "I am calling to tell you about our sale."

- *"To **reiterate** (I love this word, it gets the customer's attention every time) the purpose of my call is,"* rather than "as I said, I am calling to."

- *"My purpose in calling is to make sure you have the right products, at the right time, at the right prices and in the right place,"* rather than "I am just calling to see if you need anything."

- *"I am calling to assist you in adding some great items to your current mix of products,"* rather than "seeing how our products are doing and if you need anything."

With scripting you'll avoid some common traps and get in the habit of making productive sales calls. I purposefully call all my customers regularly to learn what they are doing to proactively improve their business and to share what others are doing to increase sales and combat whatever challenges they may face. That's better than saying, "just calling to check to see if you need anything?"

Never use the word "if" as in "to see if you need anything." It is always to learn **_what_** you need. "I just wanted to call" is past tense. It is amazing how many salespeople use this awful statement.

Always listen and review how you can better express yourself in a way that differentiates you from the common sales consultant. Develop and use _uncommon language and phrases_.

The good news is that you have so many resources to use in improving your vocabulary, starting with Google. I bet you can think of plenty of other common words that are overused.

As Jeff Bezos has been quoted saying, "leave out *weasel* words like,

un, um, yea, just wanted to, see if, and there are many more." There are more insights from Bezos in the book *The Bezos Blueprint*, by Carmine Gallo. It is about great communication from the world's greatest sales consultant, and he is pretty rich also.

Bunch's Tips
To Success:

1. Practiced scripts make my voice intonation, speaking style and flow sound professional.
2. Every phone call is an interruption, even if a family member is calling. You have about 10 to 15 seconds to answer three questions in the customer's mind.
3. Always listen and review how you can better express yourself in a way that differentiates you from the common sales consultant.

Chapter 16

Applying The Three P's Model In Your Communication

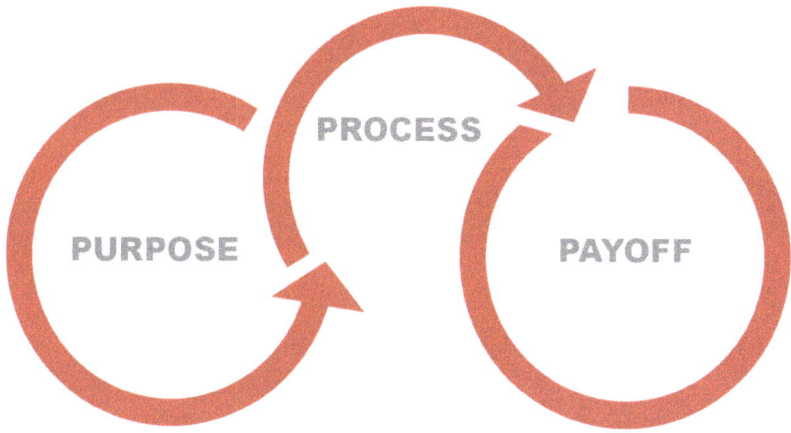

We use The Three P's model—Purpose, Process and Payoff—as our frame around everything we set out to accomplish in the sales process. These Three P's frame what we want to accomplish with our prospects/customers in a very organized and precise manner. This also applies to meetings and speeches.

The Purpose:

The *Purpose* is the specific task we want to accomplish. It is not vague or based on happenstance. The *Purpose* is what we want to accomplish from making the call or having a meeting. Therefore, our Purpose must be clear to us before we can transmit it to anyone else. What we want to accomplish must be thought out and written down. Then practice saying it until it sounds like your natural self.

Purpose states the **agenda** so that you and the customers/audience are quickly on the same page. It is designed to get you and the customer engaged in a business conversation.

Be prepared to be uncomfortable when you first use scripts since they are new and unnatural in the beginning. You will be practicing with prospects who have requested information and are excited to hear from you. Over a short period of time, you will wonder how you ever accomplished anything before you discovered the power of planning and scripting what you set out to accomplish.

Keep working with scripts/outlines until they are second nature to you. Always be prepared and never just *wing* it...even in casual calls to friends and family.How to define your **Purpose**:

1. You need to write out in one sentence the purpose/reason of what you want to accomplish from the call. Be specific:

   • I want to make a sale.

   • I want to make an appointment to make a presentation in order to move to making a sale.

   • I want to share important information with the customer.

   • I want the customer to go through the catalogue with me.

   • I want to learn what my customer is selling.

   • I want to learn more about my customers.

2. Write the script that will get your message across to the customer in an organized, easy-to-follow manner. It is what you want them to do or remember. You may have to rewrite it several times before it begins to work for you the majority of the time. Test drive it on several calls before you change it. The script has to make sense to two people: you and the customer/person you are calling.

3. A script becomes the *agenda* and keeps you focused on your desired outcome. It is not something you read to the customer. Think of it as key points you must make in an organized manner. Practice so that you can deliver it in your conversational tone and style of speaking. After all, it is what you want to accomplish and they are your words, just better organized!

> "Use The Three P's in preparing for a phone call, a meeting, a speech and for a sales presentation."

4. You always use the word ***Purpose of my call*** which sets the agenda in the customer's mind so that they are more likely to listen to you. It also avoids any false expectations in the customer's mind about the purpose of the call. It gets their attention because it is not a commonly used word in the selling process. Stating a purpose up front and then staying on script also builds trust. It is **transparent** and appreciated by the customers.

5. You can have more than one purpose but be sure to share this with the customer. Many salespeople state a purpose and then switch to one more thing. If you have two or three purposes, then state them. I have three purposes for calling: 1. To learn how your weekend sales were; 2. To share some success from other stores; 3. To share some new items for your consideration.

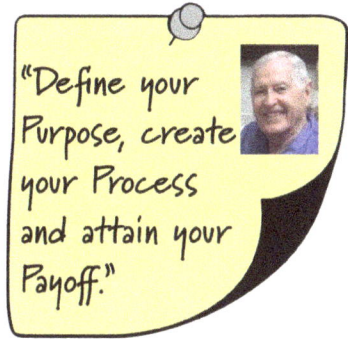

> "Define your Purpose, create your Process and attain your Payoff."

The Process:

The *Process* is how you are going to deliver your message. It is the action part of the call. Here are some guidelines in the delivery of your Purpose.

1. After stating the purpose or purposes for calling, then engage the customer in a conversational manner to direct him/her to what you want them to do/accomplish. Review every call after you make it and make any changes that you feel will make it better. You want to have a business discussion about their business and share what you can do for them.

2. Make the calls using the script you have prepared for your purpose/payoff and if it works, keep using it. If not, then adjust it until you get the results you want a high majority of the time. There are examples that you can study as a guideline a little later in this chapter.

3. Try contacting and talking with at least 10 people before you make radical changes to your script. In the beginning, be prepared to encounter push back from the customers. They may say "just send me an email." Practice overcoming this by saying "to reiterate, the purpose of this call is" and restate the purpose. You will become more comfortable and accomplished at engaging the customer and controlling the call as you practice.

4. If you repeatedly hear the same push backs, begin to make a list of those issues, and prepare your answers so that you always sound smooth and professional in your response. This helps eliminate the "ums" and hesitations.

5. Remember, you are always practicing. *The Process is the delivery of the Purpose.*

6. Always work with a mirror in front of you so that you can see how you sound. It is hard to sound stern when you smile and just as easy to forget to smile.

The Payoff:

Your *Payoff* is the desired outcome you wish to accomplish from the customer. It is accomplishing the purpose of the call. You either accomplished your Purpose or you did not.

1. You completed the call, and the customer gave you the information you requested. She said, "Thanks for calling, and I wrote down where you are at market, and I will stop by." You accomplished your Purpose.

2. You have accomplished your Payoff when the customer does what you instructed: placed an order, made an appointment, reviewed the catalogue with you or wrote down instructions on what you wanted them to do in the very near future.

"A self-coaching exercise. Before each call ask, 'why am I calling.' After the call ask, 'did I accomplish my Purpose? 'If I had that call to do over, what would I do or say differently?'"

3. A great checking/learning exercise after each call is to

ask yourself *"If I had that call to do over again what, if anything, would I change?* This is a self-coaching exercise to monitor and improve without criticizing yourself. Do this even if you accomplished your purpose. This helps reinforce your scripting skills. Train yourself to listen closely to what you are saying and to the customer's reply so that you can properly evaluate the call. That's because you will have the exact call again with another customer. Be prepared for the next time.

4. Practice your listening skills. Practice not making casual remarks like, "oh that's great." "yeah, yeah." "wonderful." These are unnecessary fillers (weasel words) that are disruptive to the person you are calling and to you who is trying to listen to what they are saying. These fillers are casual and un-business like. You would not be casual if you were calling the CEO of a Fortune 500 company so why would you be with your customer?

If you did not accomplish your Purpose or Payoff, then adjust/change your script, your voice inflections or your Purpose or the desired outcome you are after. It is very simple: if you do not get what you are after, then change and adjust until you begin getting what you set out to accomplish a high percentage of the time.

And don't forget: Always thank a customer for speaking with you: "I really appreciate your time or your order."

Scripting is a road map to get you and the customer to arrive at the same place at the same time. In the following pages, I will be sharing some scripting examples to help you achieve your desired outcomes.

Always remember you get better as you practice and coach yourself. With practice and making a lot of calls, you begin to accomplish your Purpose and Payoff a high percentage of the time and most importantly you will discover the power of controlling the conversations and accomplishing what you set out to do in less time while having the customer appreciate you.

Always ask yourself: Did I accomplish my Purpose?

For those of you who may be using this book for training, I recommend sharing with your customers that your company has made an investment to train you in products, skills and techniques to better serve the needs of our customers.

You can share with them, "This team has been trained in all aspects of our products and services to always bring you up to date information on the best performing products and industry trends. We have been trained to help our customers choose and sell the right products, at the right price and at the right time. I am pleased to have been chosen and trained for this position.

"As a product expert and your direct contact, you are my first and only concern. I will be working with you just like a road rep except rather than calling on you in person, we will work together by phone using our website and emails. You will discover that this is quick, more efficient...and fun."

Bunch's Tips
To Success:

1. Understand and embrace the power of The Three P's and use this formula in preparing for success.

2. Once you experience the power of writing scripts you will wonder how you ever existed without them.

3. Always start your calls with "the purpose of my call is."

Chapter 17

Examples Of How To Write A Script

L et's start with telephone scriptwriting for non-active customers. These are marketing calls.

Purpose:
- Create interest to revisit our company. Reconnect with customers and learn if they are still in the gift and home accessory business (or your type of business). If not, or if the phone is disconnected (check number on Google), deactivate them. Do they receive our catalogue or have access to our website?

- Introduce the new in-house service and explain how it works and how you will be working with them as a direct company contact.

- Get them to agree to an overview with you of the website or catalogue of the best products for their area; and give them webpage access.

Process:
- State the purpose of the call.

- Let the customer know about catalogue/screen-share review and set up the time.

- Share the success of products and customer successes since he/she last purchased.

Payoff:
- Qualify and clean up territory and reinstate a customer.

- Accomplish your purpose.

- Move closer to making a sale.

And now, those script examples mentioned earlier. Let's start with opening questions to build rapport in marketing. In a marketing call the purpose of these statements and questions is to help transition into a conversation to build a business rapport. Rather than asking all of the following questions, pick a few to ask the customer and then hold the rest to ask the customer during the next call. Make it natural, conversational and slow paced.

Remember, marketing calls are non-sales calls. The majority of customers will spend a few minutes discussing their business or learning something new.

You always lead with, "Hello this is (name) from the *marketing* department of (your company)."

Here are a few examples that will be helpful in preparing for your marketing calls:

1. "The purpose of my call is to learn if you are still in the _____ business."

2. "The purpose of my call is to gather some general retail information; this is not a sales call so we both can relax."

3. "The purpose of my call is to learn what special or unusual things you are doing to promote your business: sales, Facebook or special events?"

4. "The purpose of my call is learn what specific items are selling for you or if you are selling many different items."

5. "The purpose of my call is to bring your attention back to (your company), a vendor you have purchased from in the past. Do you recall purchasing from (company)?"

Many companies purchase industry lists and make cold calls. A script works well for cold calling. Review and use what you are comfortable asking and then build your own scripts for each purpose you would be calling. Share with everyone what works for you. This will help you relax and gain valuable information from the customer's current experiences.

The following outline shows you how to prepare a script followed by a blank outline that you can copy and

"Purpose, Process, Payoff."
"Make it natural, conversational and slow paced."

practice writing out scripts for different purposes.

A well scripted phone call or in-person visit has three parts:

1. A beginning that states the Purpose of the call.

2. A middle where you make your presentation is the Process.

3. An ending where you accomplish your Payoff.

You write out each of these three scripted parts. Between each of these three parts are unscripted conversations with the customer/prospect. As you begin to learn important points about your customers, you can add talking points at the bottom of your scripted call so that you always sound confident and at ease when they ask the hard questions.

CALL WORKSHEET—USING THE "THREE P's" AND "MAY I"

Write out the purpose of the call
"What do I want to happen"
I am calling to_____

_____

_____

_____

Write out the Process/
Script to accomplish your purpose:
Hello, the purpose of my call is

_____

_____

_____

Desired Payoff: What do you want to happen?
You accomplish what you set out to accomplish!
You want to:_____

_____

_____

After the call, always ask yourself, "did I accomplish my Purpose/Payoff"? Yes? No?
"If I had that call to do over again, what, if anything, would I say or do differently"?
Make note of any changes and call the next customer!

Bunch's Tips To Success:

1. A good script has three parts: A beginning that is the Purpose of the call; A middle where you make your presentation is the Process. An ending where you accomplish your Payoff.

2. As you begin to learn about your customers, add talking points so you always sound confident and at ease when they ask the hard questions.

3. A script works well for cold calling.

Part Four Summary

1. We use scripts because we sound professional, they are better for selling over the phone, they free up your mind so that you can focus on your message, they work best for repetitive calling and you never have to worry about what to say.

2. The purpose of training is to teach selling skills and techniques that have proven to get results in the shortest amount of time.

3. It is very important to develop a good descriptive vocabulary acquired through reading.

4. The Three P's model frames everything you want to accomplish. Purpose: why you are calling. Process: how you are to say what you need to say. Payoff: accomplishing what you intended to accomplish. The Three P's are a road map to get you and the customer to arrive at the same place at the same time.

5. Understand how different scripts serve different purposes: Marketing calls to bring inactive customer back; Invitation to market calls; Aftermarket calls; Calls to get an order or reorder.

Part Five

Practice Writing Your Scripts

Chapter 18

Putting It All To Use In Your Scripts

Get to work using your call worksheet

OK, it's time to get into the details by learning how to use scripts on your sales calls. This is really hands-on now, so it's up to you to use what you've learned so far and put it to good use. And don't forget to use The "Three P's" and your "May I" skills.

OUTLINE FOR MAKING CALLS USING THE "THREE P's" AND "MAY I":

Write out the Purpose of the call? What do I want to happen?

I am calling to: _____

_____

_____

_____

_____

Write out the Process/script to accomplish your Purpose.

Hello, the Purpose of my call is

_____

_____

_____

_____

Desired Payoff: What you want to happen? You accomplished what you set out to accomplish.

You want to: _____ _____

_____

_____

_____

After every call, always ask yourself, *"Did I accomplish my Purpose/Payoff"? Yes or no? "If I had that call to do over again, what, if anything, would I say or do differently?"* Make note of any changes you want to make, add, or subtract from your script and then call the next customer.

The above exercise is not a negative exercise. You do this with good calls too so that you will remember what you did well.

Examples of Marketing Calls to Reactivate Inactive Customers

You'll notice that scripts are double spaced for ease of reading. You can also mark in yellow every other line which helps you stay on script. You can do spacing and yellow marking if you have your script on your computer (you should have two screens), which is preferred, or written out and mounted where you can easily see it. An inexpensive 8X11 clear plastic "L" frame is ideal.

From the beginning you must get into the habit of saying "Hello, may I speak with" which is professional sounding. Get out of the bad habit of saying "Hi," which is casual and non-business sounding or things like is "Mary there?" or "I am trying to catch up with Mary."

> "Unpreparedness always comes through and is obvious to prospects and customers. Being and sounding disorganized blows your second chance."

Also notice that we never say, "Hello, how are you" even after you have established a relationship with the customer. Believe it or not this really aggravates a businessperson. It is also the first opportunity for the person to say, *"I am fine, I am busy and can't talk now, goodbye."* You see, since you have not stated your purpose, you are interrupting them, and they do not know why you are calling. I will admit that this is hard to do since we all have had it instilled in us to be nice.

It is not rude to get to the point in a business call.

There have been many articles in the business press interviewing CEOs who have stated that the one thing that turns them off immediately is "Hello, how are you?" The CEOs will say that they don't care how you are, and they know that you don't care how they are.

Let's get started with these scripts. This is an example of how I do a marketing call to an inactive customer in the gift and home accessory industry.

Script # 1

The Beginning:

Hello, may I speak with _____? Hello _____This is Austin from the Marketing Department of (company name), a vendor that you purchased from in the past. Do you recall (company)?

The ***Purpose*** of my call is to apologize for losing contact and to bring your attention back to (company). May I ask, are you still selling (products) gifts, seasonal, garden and home decor items?

The Middle:

(Customer's name) I would like to invite you to visit our website to discover our many new collections and products since your last purchase.

May I send you an email with a link to our website? May I verify your email address? Is it _____? Please look for someone from our sales department to follow up with you in the next couple of days to learn your interest and answer your questions.

The Ending:

(Customer's name), do you have a few moments to share a little bit about your business and product mix? (Detail, type of customer— price entry/moderate/better, location, markets and other vendors, store size).

How long have you had your business. (name), thank you for your time, have a great day!

You can always make notes below your script to help you ask important questions of the customer that will help you on your future sales call to them.

Some examples from the gift and home accessory industry:

• May I ask, who are some of your important vendors?

• How would you describe your price points–entry/moderate/better, is there a particular retail price point that works well for you?

- Do you attend any shows?

- May I ask how long you have been in business?

- May I share how we work with you? I will meet you on our website using screen share, where I will give you a quick guided tour of what we are currently doing. This first view is simply an overview and not a sales call. May I schedule a 15-minute time with you?

Next is when the buyer is not available:

Script #2

Always listen to who answers the phone and write down their name. If the buyer is not available, then use the person's name who answered the phone to ask the following:

The Beginning:

May I ask when he/she will be available?

(I do not recommend leaving a message other than) *this is just a courtesy call to share some information with him/her and to gain his/her feedback.*

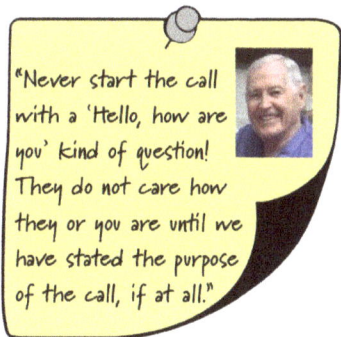

"Never start the call with a 'Hello, how are you' kind of question! They do not care how they or you are until we have stated the purpose of the call, if at all."

May I ask (use name of person that answered the phone), is he/she still the buyer of home decor gifts (your products)?

The Middle:

If not, then get the first and last name of the new buyer, an email address and make sure this is the number at which he/she can be reached.

The Ending:

If you get a pushback from the person on the phone, simply say, "I am one of his/her vendors and have some important information to share and just want to make sure he/she is still the buyer for this department. May I ask when he/she is available by phone?"

Next is an example of inviting an inactive customer to screen share:

And remember NEVER start the call with a "Hello, how are you?" kind of question! They do not care how they or you are until we have stated the purpose of the call, if at all.

Script #3.

The Beginning:

"Hello, may I speak with (name)? This is (name) with the marketing department of (company), a vendor you have purchased from in the past. The purpose of my call is to learn if you are still in the (specific industry) business and if you are still a candidate for our products. (Name) I apologize that we have lost contact with you. I would like to invite you to review (company) and update you on the many new products since you last visited us.

This is not a sales call, just an opportunity for you to view products and trends that are doing very well for our customers and to learn if we are a vendor you should revisit. It will only take a few minutes using our new screen share program.

The Middle:

May I share how this works? I will email you a link that connects us to our website and I will work with you just like a rep in your store except that I am here, and you are there. It is a quick, efficient and informative process that takes very little of your time. Do you have a few minutes to do this now? If yes, proceed. (If not) "May I schedule a 10- or 15-minute overview later today? Ok, when is a good time for you to take a break and do a quick overview?" [If they set an appointment for later]: That is a good time for me, and I have reserved that time slot for you.

The Ending:

I will email you a reminder of the time with simple instructions. May I request that you be in front of your computer for our appointment? May I verify your email?

(If not, then say) I will send you an email with my contact information and shall follow up with you in a week. Thank you for your time and consideration today. (put her on schedule for week)

Here are some delivery pointers to help you to communicate better:

- Smile! Your voice sounds friendlier. Speak at a moderate pace. Don't let the customer's first reaction speed you up.
- Be aware of your posture and sit up so you don't sound tired.
- Vary your pitch for emphasis and to maintain interest.
- Listen intently before you respond to show interest in them.
- Try not to answer in a hurried pace by pausing before you answer.
- Remember to relax. If the customer cannot talk, they will tell you.

Write Your Own Script Using Your Words (outline page 100)

OK, you've seen examples of different scripts for different types of calls so go back now and write your own script. Be prepared to share it with the group or record it on your phone for your review.

Now, let's look at scripts for invitations to your company's showroom. First, some hints and tips on how to craft your script.

Purpose:

- Extend a cordial invitation to "come see our new selections and our well merchandised showroom for ideas to use in your store."
- Share with them your success of record-breaking sales and your overall increase in our customer sales and reorders.
- Learn if they plan to attend market and, if so, how many days? If not, make the recommendation that they review our website and its many categories. List assortment of products, for example: ceramics, paintings, mirrors, clocks, pendant lamps, occasional furniture and many other gifts and home décor items that your company offers.

These items are from home accessory lines; you, of course, will need to make reference to your product categories. Set them up to view your website or confirm a time that you can guide them through a screen share.

Process:

- Using a friendly and enthusiastic manner to prompt them to include us on their must-see market calendar. Then email them the location of the showroom with your contact information. The more detailed your directions, the more likely they are to remember and to find you. Many salespeople are also texting the customer during market as a reminder to stop by.

- If they do not plan on attending the market, then recommend they do an overview with an in-house rep to learn best sellers with stores similar to theirs as well as emerging trends. This can be done using the join-me screen sharing

Payoff:

- Drive active and inactive customers to our showroom during shows.

- Generate desire for them to review and purchase our products.

- Extend goodwill and keep our name in front of them.

Now, scripting examples for those market invitations:

Script #4

The Beginning:

"Hello, may I speak with (name)?" "Hello, (name) this is (your name) with (company), the purpose of my call is to extend a cordial invitation to you to please come see us at the (name of show) in a couple of weeks (give dates). We want you to discover why our customers have given us a record of pre-market sales."

The Middle:

"(Their name) are you planning to attend _____ ___? (Yes) Will you please include us on your list of new vendors to visit?

We have many great new products and an award-winning showroom of ideas for your store merchandising. We encourage picture taking of how we display our products for maximum selling in your store. We do get busy from Friday on, so we encourage you to stop by early during the market. Thanks, (name), for your time today and I look forward to seeing you at the show." (Some customers will make appointments, and some will not. If they do, then make an appointment).

The Ending:

Please write down our showroom locations which is (you got a pen?) located in building # ___on the ___the floor at the escalator suite #_____." (You should also send email of location)

Extending the call:

Prospect says, "No, I am not going."

(Name) "May I ask, what markets do you usually attend?" Please put us on that schedule. In the meantime, we have a unique way of giving you a quick overview of our new selections. May I share that with you? I will email you a link that connects you to our website and I will work with you just like a rep in your store except I am here, and you are there. It is quick, efficient, informative and takes very little of your time. Do you have a few minutes to do this now?

If yes, proceed. If no, "May I schedule a few minutes later today? Ok, when is a good time for you to take a break, have a cup of coffee and do a quick overview?" "(name), what questions do you have for me?

Thank you, (name); I look forward to having you back as a customer!"

Now it's your turn, write your own script using your words for this situation. And don't forget to be prepared to share it with the group or record it for your review.

Next is a marketing and reorder call script. The purpose is to bring their attention back to your company and to move them closer to making an order.

"Don't jump to the defensive when a customer objects to what you're saying. Respond with more discovery."

Standard suggested scripts:

Purpose:

To arouse customer interest in ordering our products now.

"The purpose of my call is to bring (company) to your immediate attention. We are enjoying double-digit sales increases because our customers are selling our products very well and reordering our best sellers. (name) as a reminder, spring, Easter or Mother's Day is just around the corner and now is a great time to spruce up the store and bring in some great new ideas for your customers. My customers appreciate a quick overview of what is selling well, and my assisting them in creating an order. May I do a review and assist you in putting some items on an order today?"

(Put together some answers for rebuttals.)

Our next scriptwriting exercise is for making a sale. The purpose of this call is to learn what a customer has sold from a recent shipment or to place an order in general. You should:

- Encourage the customer to reorder their best sellers and add other great products.

- Share with them any incentives and why they should reorder at this time.

This is a sales call: you are demonstrating your *Value Proposition* by being proactive to what they should consider doing. You will be interacting with the customer in a positive business manner. How you come across in your wording, pace, volume and tone—casual or business-like—will be judged by who you are calling during and after the call. Customers judge all calls from reps.

Therefore, you should plan out what you want them to do and how you are going to lead/guide them to that end using the *Purpose, Process and desired Payoff model*. State your purpose and get your information and then let the customer talk about his/her business.

Customers who have received a recent shipment from your company:

Script #5

The Beginning:

Hello, may I speak with _____? Hello _____, this is _____ with the _____ (company).

The purpose of my call is to share what products you purchased, learn what you have sold and recommend some items you may want to consider reordering at this time.

(Name), you purchased these items from us: _____, _____, _____, _____.

The Middle:

May we take a moment to see which of these items you have already sold? (Name the items sold) Great, shall we reorder those exact items? (yes/no) Should we order similar items? May I share some other best-selling items that you should consider at this time? *(customer's interaction with you where you listen)*

(Send link to website or you should send link as soon as they answered the phone).

The Ending:

(Name) if you will go to your computer; I have sent you our catalogue live link that shows what you have ordered, and we can review some other considerations to keep your sales moving forward.

From here on it is a business discussion and you direct and react to where you want the conversation to go. You may write an order, or you may put things in the cart or email them recommendations to consider and call them in a couple of days to collect an order. Add pushback answers that have worked for you to the bottom of your script for quick reference.

Here's the next script, for a follow-up after a screen share presentation.

After you've demonstrated the screen share process to a customer (whether an inactive or a new customer), you will follow up to establish a date for the actual sales presentation using screen share.

Script #6

Hello, May I speak with (name)? Hello (name), this is _____ with (company). The purpose of my call is to follow up on our overview and to arrange a time that we can view (company) products for your store using the screen share app that I demonstrated to you several days ago. May we do that now?

(If not) How about later today? (Make the appointment for later today or tomorrow. (Try not to make it over a week away.)

If the customer pushes back, remind them that since you will only be showing one company that it is quick and to the point and takes less time than an in-store appointment. If the customer pushes back with "I just don't need anything now," then use one or more of the following examples:

1. We have several products that have proven to be strong sellers that you should be aware of for now or future purchases. This would be a good time to at least plan as you continue good selling.

2. Since we have not worked together, I would like to learn what your likes and dislikes are as we review our general line. May I have some time with you? It would really help me to better assist you in the future. How about early morning tomorrow?

3. I realize that reps calling on you in store can take a lot of time and make you feel obligated to buy something. Since I am a company specialist, my mission is to assist you in making the best selection for your store and not to just make a sale. If a customer comes in while we are on the phone, you can assist them and then come back to me, and we'll pick up where we left off.

4. Last resort: (Name), when may I have the pleasure of presenting (company) to you using this quick and efficient method and learning more about what you like from our large selection of products?

If he/she gives you a time, great. If not, ask for a future date or time that you may call again for an appointment.

(Name), as you know, each weekend of sales changes your needs and, with that in mind, I will call you within the next couple of weeks to find out what your needs are at that time.

Thank you for your time and consideration today. May I email you my contact information for your files?

What do you do if your customer objects to what you are saying? Don't jump to the defensive. First reiterate why you are calling and then ask questions to further understand the customer's needs and concerns, using the "May I" approach.

Don't defend or react!   Respond with more discovery!

Remember there are three things a person wants to know when you call, and they want to know them in about fifteen seconds!

1.   Who's calling me?

2.   Why are you calling me?

3.   What value is it to me to stop what I am doing, listen and engage in your call?

Bunch's Tips To Success:

1. Scripting is about the most valuable sales tool there is.

2. Use different scripts for different types of calls.

3. And don't forget: Always thank a customer for speaking with you: "I really appreciate your time."

4. Smile! Your voice sounds friendlier.

Part Five Summary

1.   We use scripts because we sound professional. They are better for selling over the phone; they free up your mind so that you can focus on your message; they work best for repetitive calling, and you never have to worry about what to say.

2.   It is very important to develop a good descriptive vocabulary acquired through reading.

3.   The Three P's model frames everything you want to accomplish. Purpose: why you are calling. Process: how you say what you need to say. Payoff: accomplishing what you intended to accomplish.

4.   The Three P's are a road map to get you and the customer to arrive at the same place at the same time.

5.   Understand how different scripts serve different purposes: Marketing calls to bring inactive customers back; Invitation to market calls; After market calls; Calls to get an order or reorder.

The In-Person Selling Experience At Markets

Chapter 19

Working Markets And Trade Shows

While we've devoted most of this book to the process of selling by phone and using virtual devices like computers, texts and emails, for many industries, in-person trade shows and markets are critical parts of the entire sales process.

But in fact, how you sell at shows, in person at an office or in a store, is remarkably similar to how you do it through tele sales. The skills and techniques you use match up well no matter where the actual selling is being done.

The Ground Rules For Markets And Trade Shows

Always be alert to customers coming in and customers in the showroom who are just looking. At any time, they may be ready to write an order. You may be visiting with other personnel but stay alert to the customer's movements and when he/she needs assistance. Be prepared to drop your conversation and answer a question or write an order. Practice being a good ambassador for your company and yourself.

New products will be displayed throughout the showrooms and blended in with last year's best sellers. There are lots of new items in every category. When you are not with a customer, walk around to see where products are located. Get in the habit of looking up and down and behind things. Know what is in the showroom and where it is located. It will take several days to know where everything is, and you will still discover products you have not seen before. Ask when you cannot find an item.

If you get a good idea of what is in each room, you can better work with your customers. If you cannot find an item, then look it up on your digital device and show the customer the product picture.

Ask your customers questions about their store and their customers. Who are their customers— budget, moderate or upscale? Who is their *average* customer? This builds your credibility with the customer and helps to direct you to what to show them in product categories and pricing and what not to show them.

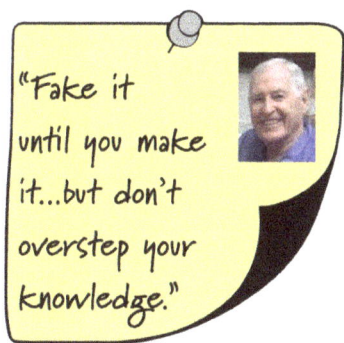

"Fake it until you make it...but don't overstep your knowledge."

Observe what they are buying and ask: "May I ask why you like this item?" When you show a well booked item, and they say no, also ask: "May I ask why it did not appeal to you?" Once you get a feel for their taste and price points, then you can make intelligent recommendations for their consideration. The customer thinks you are one of the smartest salespeople they have worked with.

As a customer shops your products, he/she asks: "what is this company's Value Proposition? What distinguishes this company from all the rest and what value does the company offer me?" Answer those questions as you work with your customer by demonstrating those values. Do not commit assume-a-sides by assuming an existing customer remembers all the values of the company.

"Our company designs and researches our products from many countries. By shopping the world, we bring a concentration of the best gift and home décor products to accent your store. This saves you time and the frustration of having to shop large selections in a crowded showroom and trying to find what we have already pre-shopped for you."

Other things to do and be aware of

1. Don't stand around in groups and close off the front door, stand to the left. Help out in traffic control. Greet everyone who enters the showroom.

2. The market temp workers can approach customers and direct customers to reps that work the area the customer is from. If everyone is busy, then the temps work the customer.

3. Anytime a customer will not give you a credit card and asks you to call them, bring them to your manager. You must have a credit card to go with an order. It saves time since it takes about three calls to get a customer on the phone. Multiply that by 1,000 and then you will see why you need to get the credit card immediately. Orders stay in purgatory until released with a credit card or approved credit. You don't do your customers any favors by not getting required credit cards or credit forms at the time the order is placed.

4. You can write two or three orders at a time. Many products are sold out before the shows are over. If you have the ability to see current availability as you sell products, then you can place another order for the next available ship date. This ensures they get everything they order at markets, and you can make reorders for the best booked items.

   "Wear comfortable shoes."

5. If you use the two-minute commercial (next chapter), know the location of new products and a little about the store you are working with, *you will write larger orders.*

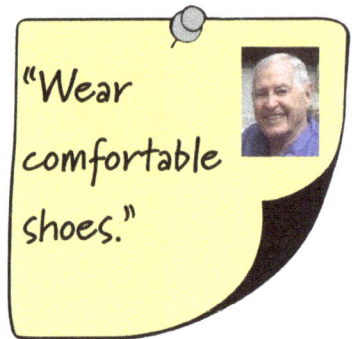

6. Observe, take notes and use what you hear and see. Everyone at the market knows something different than you. When you are in the showroom you are supposed to be a professional in the eyes of the customer. "Fake it until you make it," but don't overstep your knowledge.

7. Always ask your manager for answers you don't have. You can always interrupt the manager even if he/she is with a customer...at least you should be able to.

8. Remember when you are new and learning, that customers are accustomed to working with temps and new reps. Relax and enjoy the experience.

9. Wear comfortable shoes and bring more than one pair so that you can change during the day. This applies more to women than men. Comfort always trumps style. Also, take breaks or you will burn out before the day is done.

10. And always be prepared with your two-minute commercial. (More on that in a minute.)

A few more things to remember at Shows and Markets

1. Stress your company's uniqueness to your customers: We are company product specialists. We speak to over 200 independent customers a week. We keep customers up to date and well informed. We make sure you have the right products, at the right time, in the right place and at the right price,

2. Behavior in the markets: Learn the products, be positive and friendly and share both the company's and your Value Proposition. Observe what the customer is buying and why and what he/she is not buying and why?

3. Create and use your two-minute commercial as your marketing approach to begin the sales process.

Bunch's Tips
To Success:

1. Selling in person requires very similar skills to selling on the phone.

2. Always be alert for a customer in the showroom. Know where everything is and what are the new products.

3. If you're between sales appointments, walk around the showroom and familiarize yourself with the products.

Chapter 20

The Two-Minute Commercial For Trade Shows

Marketing precedes the sales process

This is your opening market statement or what we call a two-minute commercial. It quickly prepares the customer to view you as unique and to dispel any price comparison or misconceptions. If you do not do this with your customers before you begin your presentation, they will be making comparisons and assumptions rather than discovering great products and merchandising ideas.

I call this a two-minute commercial and I tell the customer I am only going to take 30 seconds, which is true. Works for me every time. Many customers will look at their watch and time me.

Sharing who we are and then asking customers about their business puts you and them on equal terms to begin a business presentation. It is marketing at its best. It also <u>differentiates</u> you from the masses.

Example of a general two-minute/30-second commercial:

"Hello, welcome to our showroom. May I ask, are you an existing customer? (If yes) welcome back. (Even with returning customers say: May I update you and give my two-minute overview commercial.)"

(If new) "Welcome to our showroom. We are so pleased that you have come. May I ask how you discovered us? May I share our two-minute commercial if I only take 30 seconds?" (Yes) "We are a gift (or home décor and holiday) company that has invested over __ years of creating a unique line of fun and great selling items. We cover a broad base of categories and price points.

Our products work for all types of customers, which results in successful selling for our customers.

"We employ many designers around the globe to create and source hundreds of new products. We ship in a prompt timeframe. At this market we have freight and discount specials. Our opening order is _____.

"Please tell me a little about your store and take as much time as you like." This is the customer's marketing story so listen and ask questions to gain valuable information on how to best present to his/her interests and needs. You want to learn how long they have been in business, types of products, major vendors and best price points.

(Thank them and ask) "How would you like to proceed? Would you like me to guide you around or do you want to look and then have me work with you? (If they want to look around, then say) I will check back with you from time to time to learn what questions you may have and to write your order."

> "I call this a two-minute commercial and tell the customer I am only going to take 30 seconds. Works for me every time. Many will time me."

Now, write your own two-minute commercial

Take 10 minutes and write your own two-minute/30-second commercial. Rehearse and time it to make sure you can deliver it in 30 seconds. Be prepared to practice giving it to a manager or friend for feedback.

Why have a two-minute commercial and share it with existing and new customers? Because at markets they are seeing hundreds of other vendors. Even good customers need to be refocused during a show. It also demonstrates good business etiquette.

It helps to erase all of the other shotgun approaches they have heard from other aggressive salespeople just trying to sell them something as soon as they enter the showroom. I always get a positive feedback from customers in all the different client showrooms that I have worked in the past 34 years. They always find it refreshing.

Use script #4 (see page 104) to make invites to markets and trade shows.

So, let's take a look at The Three P's and how they relate to selling in person. A simple fact about customers; they are much more relaxed and friendly when they are out of their stores and at trade shows. It is like a young mother with three toddlers who gets a five-day vacation away from the kids and daily tasks.

Purpose:

1. See the new products, interact with other salespeople and learn the showroom layout.

2. Meet with your customers and prospects to learn more about them and write large orders.

3. Get you excited and on the same page as everyone else.

4. Practice being positive, helpful and friendly to everyone.

5. Remember the customer's positive reaction to products and share that on the phone when you're back in the office.

"Everyone at market knows something different than you, so observe and ask questions of customers and salespeople."

Process:

1. Share the company's Value Proposition so that you can differentiate you and your company from the ordinary vendors by using a two-minute commercial that lasts for only 30 seconds.

2. Show, tell, make recommendations, romance the products, ask and answer questions.

3. Write lots of orders even if it is not your account.

4. Learn about the customers and what motivates them to buy or not to buy. Why do they like a product or why they do not like a product?

5. Be observant of the customer and listen to his/her comments as they look. Even when you are not working with a customer, observe customers as they work with other reps to learn how they are reacting to the products and the sales consultant's presentation.

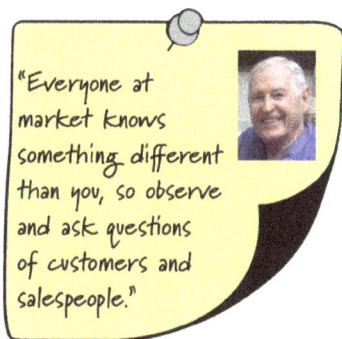

6. Thank them for their time and order and be sure to tell them **how you will be working with them between markets over the phone and with screen-share, email and texting. Please do not forget this important part**.

Payoff:

1. You and the customers become better educated in each other's company and they place larger orders. They will also be more likely to take your calls.

2. Your company, the customers and you will have a great market and successful kickoff to a great season.

3. Large market orders beget many reorders until the next market. You become more informed and excited about the products and the customers.

4. You will bring your new knowledge and experiences back to the office to share with customers on the phone and through screen sharing.

"If you know the two-minute commercial, sharing who we are and then asking customers about their business puts you and the customer on equal terms to begin a business presentation. It is marketing at its best. It also differentiates you from the masses."

5. The customer will now know that you will be working with them on the phone to follow-up between markets, write reorders and review new products.

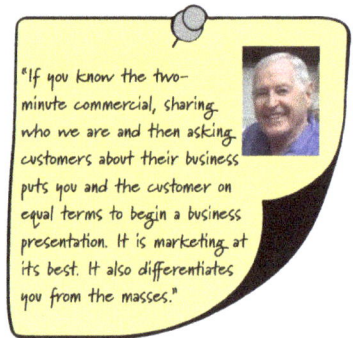

Bunch's Tips
To Success:

1. The skills and techniques you use match up well no matter where the actual selling is done.

2. Use markets to learn more about customers and their business: who are their customers, what their store is like and what trends they try to follow.

3. Observe, take notes and use what you hear and see. Everyone at the market knows something different than you.

4. Don't forget The "Three P's"...and "May I."

Part Six Summary

1. Don't stand around in groups and close off the front door, stand to the left. Help out in traffic control. Greet everyone who enters the showroom.

2. Good business etiquette is just as important at shows and markets as it is on the phone.

3. Comfort always trumps style. Wear comfortable shoes and bring more than one pair so that you can change during the day.

Part Seven

The End...But Really Only The Beginning

Chapter 21

Where We've Been

W ay back in the first few pages of this book, the whole concept
of being a good sales consultant was just that...a concept. But
we've traveled a fascinating journey that has taken us from that stage
through defining what exactly is selling, using data to make a sale,
training, communications, scriptwriting and working in-person to arrive at becoming a true sales specialist.

This book is your study guide, your reference to use on an ongoing
basis and refer to when you need a refresher course, feel you've lost
your way or just want the affirmation that you're doing it right.

So, a few last tools you can use before we finish up.

**Introspection, Self-management and Self-coaching for Self-im-
provement**

---

1. **When your presentation quits working for you, what
do you do?**

- First, you have to be aware that it is not working before
you are too far into your day, so review yourself in time
to reverse the trend. This comes from paying attention to
and reviewing each call as discussed earlier.

- Monitor yourself to obtain the results you want from the
customer: to be responsive and to take action. In other
words, are you getting orders on the phone, emailed or on
the web?

- Ask yourself, "Am I getting the maximum results I want?
Am I really focused on what I am doing?" "Did I accomplish my purpose?" and "If I had that call to do over again
what, if anything, would I change?

- Increase your number of calls or switch to marketing calls
to break up your day.

2. Evaluate your "assumptions."

- Are you focused on what you want to accomplish?

- Are you tripping up yourself by thinking, "I have sold everyone and no one else is interested?"

- Are you committing assume-a-sides? Have you stopped using the process of The Three P's?

- Are you always using "May I" when asking questions?

- Has a series of calls or customers made you negative or beaten you down?

- Have you rethought what you want to accomplish from your calls?

- Are you thinking from the customer's perspective? What do they want/need?

- Have you reviewed your numbers for the day and made a plan of how you are going to meet your standards for the day?

- Are you practicing good listening skills and using your script?

3. You are the boss of you.

- You are the manager of your time, task, territory, dollars and attitude.

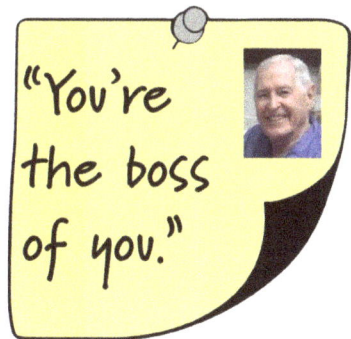

"You're the boss of you."

- Are you aware that you are writing your commission check daily? You are creating the sales consultant that you will become.

- Are you putting quality time into you? Are you following the guidelines of what you have been trained to do?

4. Are you creating value?

- Are you developing your territory and training your customers that you are a real value to them and will grow their business?

- Ask yourself, "What does my customer think of me?" "Would I take my call if I were the customer?"

5. **Are you putting in a full day of selling?**

- Are you really concentrated on accomplishing the set standards and reaching beyond to your own goals?

- Are you quitting before the job is done?

- Do you feel you are growing and learning in your job?

6. **Are you making a daily plan of how you are going to reach your standards?**

- Do you have a strategy of who you are calling, what you want to sell them and what you want them to do? Is it clear to you and the customer/prospect?

- Are you using the three hours of focused calling and four hours of planning and other tasks or are you mixing up your day going back and forth between calling and other tasks?

- Are you focused on one task at a time?

Bunch's Tips To Success:

1. Know what to do when your presentation skills stop working.
2. Always evaluate your assumptions.
3. Make sure you are truly making the best use of your time.

Chapter 22

Every Day We Invest In Tomorrow

Every day we prepare for tomorrow, next week and next year. Every activity and thought is processed and stored for future use. We are consciously and sub-consciously acquiring thoughts, ideas, results, inspirations, positive and negative feedback that prepare us to face the next day and future days, in our work and personal life.

Are we in control of these events? Can we take control of these events? We should ask ourselves the following questions:

1. Before good habits can be developed, you must first develop discipline. Am I disciplined?

2. What kind of person do I want to be in my professional and personal life?

3. What can I do to filter out the negative thoughts and unproductive activities?

4. Can I control my thoughts, actions and reactions professionally?

5. Do I write down and read my goals and things I want to change daily?

6. Do I leave home and leave personal issues at home?

> "Every day we are preparing for tomorrow, next week and next year."

7. Do I put in a full day of work utilizing good planning and execution of my time and talents? Do I leave work feeling good about the day and leave work issues at work?

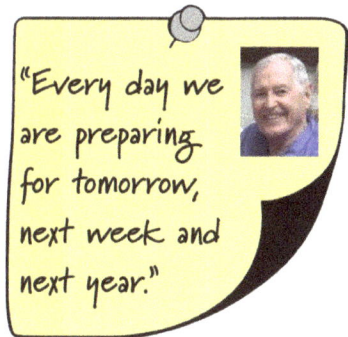

8. Am I investing in having a good day at work by having a good evening at home? Do I eat right, relax and sleep well so I am refreshed for the next day?

9. Do I realize on Sunday that tomorrow is a workday and plan accordingly?

10. Am I assessing my habits to weed out the non-productive ones and replacing them with positive pro-active habits?

11. Do I feel I can improve in my professional position?

12. Am I a good example to my co-workers and the company?

13. Am I open minded to changing and improving? Can I develop a proactive mindset?

Bunch's Tips To Success:

1. Self-management and Self-coaching are critical for Self-improvement.
2. Focus on one thing at a time.
3. You are the boss of you. You are the manager of your time, task, territory, dollars and attitude and are writing your commission check daily. You are creating the sales consultant that you will become.

Chapter 23

Let's Review Where You Started And Where You Are As A Sales Specialist Now

1. You started with the basics of marketing by calling on new and existing customers and exchanging general information about the company and asking questions from the customers.

2. You learned more about your company, the industry and the customers you will be calling.

3. You learned about *Purpose, Process and Payoff* and how to always prepare before any call, presentation, or meeting. You should now be using this process on every call...always.

4. You will do several weeks of comfort calling, calling dormant customers to see if they are still in business and a candidate for your products. This is practicing.

5. You studied and learned the value of "Social Styles" to learn more about different styles of people and how to react to each to maximize your newly learned selling skills. You used the selling skills of *Purpose, Process and Payoff* to get customers' attention and deliver your message in a short, effective amount of time.

6. You will spend several months practicing your newly learned skills by calling customers and prospects and taking orders when the customer says, "Oh, I need to place an order."

7. You practiced, practiced and practiced your newly developed skills. You will have numerous breakout sessions daily to review

"Forget mistakes. Forget failures. Forget everything except what you're going to do now and do it. Today is your lucky day."
-- Will Durant.

147

your progress and hear each other's successes and learn from each other, the customer, and the manager.

8. You will move from passive calling and information gathering to skilled selling and asking for orders.

9. You will be attending major markets and learning: The products show very well, customers are easy to talk with, customers are easy to begin writing orders with, customers listen and respond to what you have to say.

10. You have come a long way in a short period of time. You have learned more than a lot of long-term salespeople who have learned by trial and error. You will be selling against "old school" salespeople who do not have the current skills and techniques that you now possess.

11. You are good at markets and on the phone. You now will move to be an expert in selling and even on to territory and account management.

12. Now, go and grow in you craft.

Bunch's Tips To Success:

1. We have to say it again: Purpose, Process, Payoff. Repeat until you get it.
2. Did we mention that "May I" are the two most important words you can use in any conversation.
3. Now, go and grow your craft.

Chapter 24

Recommended Readings

We've covered a lot of territory in this book but there's always more to read. I believe that you are always improving and learning. Selling is a "Practice," at least for those who continue to improve skills, techniques and earnings.

So, here's a sampling of some great business, marketing, and sales books I have read that I suggest you check out:

1. *Building A StoryBrand, Clarify Your Message So Customers Will Listen*, by Donald Miller

2. *Pitch Perfect, How to Say It Right the First Time, Every Time*, by Bill McGowan

3. *The Challenger Sale, Taking Control of the Customer Conversation*, by Matthew Dixon and Brent Adamson.

4. *The One Thing, The Surprisingly Simple Truth Behind Extraordinary Results*, by Gary Keller

5. *To Sell Is Human, The Surprising Truth About Moving Others*, by Daniel H. Pink

6. *Smarter Faster Better, The Secrets Of Being Productive In Life and Business,* by Charles Duhigg

7. *Perennial Seller, The Art Of Making and Marketing Work That Lasts*, by Ryan Holiday

8. *5% More: Making Small Changes To Achieve Extraordinary Results*, by Michael Alden

9. *Competing Against Luck: The Story Of Innovation and Customer Choice*, by Clayton M. Christensen

10. *Selling Boldly*, by Alex Goldfayn

11. *You're Not Listening*, by Kate Murphy

12. *Exactly What to Say*, by Phil M. Jones

13. *Deep Work*, by Cal Newport

14. *Never Split the Difference*, by Chris Voss

15. *Atomic Habits*, by James Clear

16. *Think Again*, by Adam Grant

17. *Peak Mind*, by Amishi P. Jha, PhD

18. *Indistractable*, by Nir Eyal.

19. *QBQ! The Question behind the Questions*, by John G. Miller

20. *Selling With Noble Purpose*, by Lisa Earle McLeod with Elizabeth Lotardo

21. *The Earned Life, Lose Regret, Choose Fulfillment*, by Marshall Goldsmith

22. *The Disruption Mindset, why some organizations transform while others fail*, by Charlene Li

23. *Smart Brevity*, by Jim VandeHei, Mike Allen & Roy Schwartz

24. *The Bezos Blueprint*, by Carmine Gallo

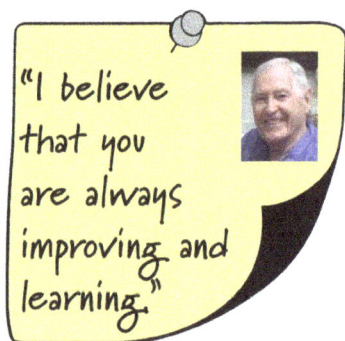

"I believe that you are always improving and learning."

Bonus Reading on Philosophy

1. *Tribe of Mentors, Short Life Advice from the Best in the World*, by Timothy Ferriss

2. *Man's Search for Meaning*, by Viktor E. Frankl

3. *The Alchemist*, by Paulo Coelho

4. *The Four Agreements, A Toltec Wisdom Book*, by Don Miguel Ruiz

5. *Grit, The Power of Passion and Perseverance*, by Angela Duckworth

6. *Think and Grow Rich*, by Napoleon Hill

7. *The Power of Positive Thinking*, by Dr. Norman Vincent Peale

8. *Mindset*, by Carol Dweck.

9. *Search Inside Yourself*, by Chade-Meng Tan

10. *The Subtle Art of Not Giving A F*ck*, by Mark Manson

11. *Thinking, Fast and Slow*, by Daniel Kahneman

12. *21 Lessons for the 21st Century*, by Yuval Noah Harari

13. *Discipline is Destiny, Power of Self-Control*, by Ryan Holiday

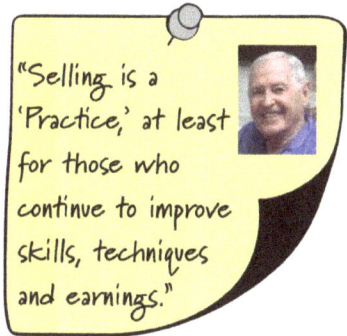

"Selling is a 'Practice,' at least for those who continue to improve skills, techniques and earnings."

REMINDERS!

"New skills and knowledge are of little value unless we put them to use daily and improve upon them."

A quote by Austen Bunch

Sales Process Funnel

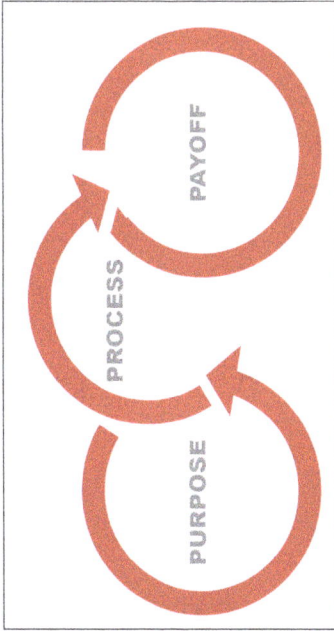

CALLS / DIALED

30% Completed

50% to Presentations

30% BUY

Sales Made

#of Sales = Dollars
Amount of each sale = Total $$

480 Minutes (8 Hours)

PAYOFF

PROCESS

PURPOSE

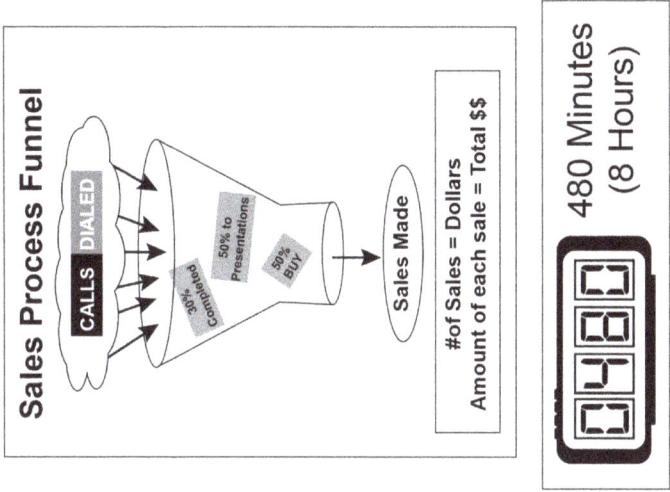

MAY I

CAN I

Discovery and Scripting

Cut out and put on your wall!

153

www.ingramcontent.com/pod-product-compliance
Lightning Source LLC
Chambersburg PA
CBHW041912190326
41458CB00023B/6241